ΛPPΛLΛCHIΛN
R E V I E W

VOL. 48, NO. 3
SUMMER 2020

TRADITION. DIVERSITY. CHANGE.

EDITOR
Jason Kyle Howard

BOOK REVIEWS EDITOR
Emily Masters

STUDENT ASSISTANTS
Skylar Bensheimer & Christopher Stuchell

MANUSCRIPT READERS
Katherine Scott Crawford & Patti Frye Meredith

ESTABLISHED IN 1973
PUBLISHED QUARTERLY
by Berea College
CPO 2166
205 N. Main Street
Berea, Kentucky 40404
www.appalachianreview.net

The short stories in this publication are works of fiction. Names, characters, places, and incidents are either the products of the authors' imaginations or are used fictitiously. Any resemblance to actual events, locales, or persons, living or dead, is entirely coincidental. The views expressed in the creative nonfiction herein are solely those of the authors.

Electronic submissions only at www.appalachianreview.net

Distributed by the University of North Carolina Press. Basic subscription price: $30/year for individuals, $40/year for institutions. For subscription requests and inquiries, visit the magazine's website, email uncpress_journals@unc.edu, or call 919.962.4201.

CONTENTS

EDITOR'S NOTE..*Jason Kyle Howard*   6

FICTION

Mark Powell

    Market Forces...   9

Sheila R. Lamb

    The Spring...   80

CREATIVE NONFICTION

Kathleen Driskell

    Keats in the Time of Your Pandemic.................................... 35

Angela Jackson-Brown

    Where Have All the Safety Pins Gone?............................... 68

POETRY

Jason B. Crawford

    Untitled 3 (Tanna).. 31

    Ghouls... 32

    Elephant in the Burning Dress.. 33

    Orchard... 34

Ansel Elkins

    The Race Bone... 49

John Q. Mars

    honey boy, honey boy 60

    a pedagogical love 64

    Hoochstroke 66

Benjamin Cutler

    The River 75

    Elegies of Gathering 76

    Self-Portrait as Fly Fisherman 78

    Devil's Walking Stick 79

Emry Trantham

    Carolina Parakeet 92

    Lakeside 94

    The White Moth 96

    Touch Me Not 97

Laura Long

    Hope Is a Thing Before Feathers 105

Eileen Elizabeth

    Damson 106

Melva Sue Priddy

    What I Couldn't Give Her 118

    The Kitchen, Empty 119

INTERVIEW

Jason Kyle Howard

    Ansel Elkins 51

CRAFT ESSAY

Jessie van Eerden

    This Present Absence: The Generative Power of
    Epistolary Form 98

BOOK REVIEWS

Jayne Moore Waldrop
At the Center of All Beauty: Solitude and the Creative Life by Fenton Johnson... 107

Donna M. Crow
The Giver of Stars by Jojo Moyes and *The Book Woman of Troublesome Creek* by Kim Michele Richardson.......... 110

Katie Mitchell
Fatherless: A Memoir by Keith Maillard............................ 115

CONTRIBUTORS 120

COVER PHOTOGRAPH

Satsumas with Leaves by Amanda Greene

EDITOR'S NOTE

JASON KYLE HOWARD

T he years changed things; destroyed things; heaped things up—worries and bothers; here they were again," Virginia Woolf writes in *The Years*, the story of a family in London navigating the changes wrought by nearly sixty successive years of loss, family tensions, political strife, war, and heartache. True to life, some of the characters find themselves encountering the same issues over and over again in subtle acts of eternal recurrence. Some are liberated, while others feel trapped, caught in one of time's wrinkles.

The pandemic has sometimes made me feel that way. Time has stood curiously still. And then it feels as if we are moving in warp speed, with a velocity that is fast and jarring, before things slow again to a near standstill. Some days are mind-numbingly the same; others have offered a measure of variety. One of my constants, of course, has been reading, and I have found myself returning to some of my favorite authors, such as Woolf and James Baldwin, for stability and wisdom.

I hope this issue of *Appalachian Review* can provide some of that same anchoring. "Market Forces," an excerpt from an upcoming novel by Mark Powell, examines the effects of ecoterrorism on an Appalachian town. Sheila R. Lamb's short story "The Spring" brims with mystery and is enchanting in every sense of the word. The two essays featured here—"Keats in the Time of Your Pandemic" by Kathleen Driskell and "Where Have All the Safety Pins Gone?" by Angela Jackson-Brown—each manage a remarkable feat. Timely, rooted in our present moment, they are also enduring, carrying themes and meanings that are perpetual in nature. Likewise, poetry by Jason B. Crawford, Benjamin Cutler, Emry Trantham, John Q. Mars, Melva Sue Priddy, Laura Long, and Eileen Elizabeth offer exquisite moments of lyricism, grief, and beauty. We are proud to feature a new poem from Ansel Elkins, winner of the 2014 Yale Younger Poets Prize, who also reflects on her poetry and teaching in an insightful conversation. Jessie van Eerden, author of the forthcoming epistolary novel *Call It Horses*, explores the enduring resonance of the form in her craft essay "This Present Absence."

Our current year has certainly changed and destroyed things. It has heaped things up, revealing disparities and inequities that have long been ignored, that must be confronted and changed. We can make it, I am convinced, by being responsible in our everyday lives. By wearing our masks. By listening—by hearing and heeding the cries for justice. And by allowing the power of stories, to paraphrase Ansel Elkins, to expand our souls. ∎

MARKET FORCES

MARK POWELL

She drove down on a glorious May morning, and had she not already known she was leaving God's country she would have suspected she was entering it. Kathryn Banks had woke in an angle of light, the early sun falling through the bedroom window of her Loudon County estate and, for the first time since her husband had passed away the previous June, felt what might be called happiness or, if not happiness, purpose. Her daughters were away for the weekend, Maddy a junior at Hollins, Jocelyn, a high school sophomore, sleeping at a friend's, so Kathryn walked alone through the paddocks and out to the stables. The horses appeared as luminous as the day, though she suspected that was simply the product of her mood. She had coffee and spent twenty minutes doing a serious of intense body weight exercises (planks, pushups, bicycle kicks—she had an app on her phone) and another twenty in the half lotus, attuning her breath. She showered and dressed, matched a Hermes scarf to her Eileen Fisher pants, and, sometime around eight, got in her Lexus and started south on I-81.

The bottling plant lay on 176 acres in a forgotten corner of Southwest Virginia, rolling hills, grazing Herefords. Farther east began the coalfields, the gutted seams and striated rock, but that was miles away. Here it was all apple orchards and bike trails, the farm-to-table restaurants by the clapboard churches, and beneath it all, a water as pure as the day.

Credit card receipts indicate she stopped once for gas and bottle of Lion Heart Kombucha (BEV $4.19) in Wytheville.

Cellular records indicate she made no phone calls.

It was just after lunch when she met the realtor, Monty Drudge, at his downtown office in Mountain View. His office, like the town, might be described as fabricated quaint. A fish-scaled Victorian, it had Federalist furniture and a La Marzocco espresso machine. The town had gaslights and a microbrewery. All of it intentional—the shabby chic the product of a Richmond consultancy—and all of it animated by the sort of civic pride that arises at the intersection of affluence and affectation.

Though he acted as if he knew nothing of her, Drudge admitted in later court findings he had done a minimum of due diligence, which is to say he had Googled Kathryn Banks. So, as they sat down to coffee and croissants on the wrought iron chairs in the triangle of courtyard behind his office—it really was a glorious day, all peonies and sunlight—Drudge would have known that when her husband had died the previous summer of a heart attack outside the U.S. District Court in Oakland, California, he had left his wife with sole ownership of a water bottling consortium that stretched from Rialto, California, to Enterprise, Florida, and was valued at roughly 147 million US dollars (Mr. Banks had consistently disputed this figure, thus his appearance that day in court). Drudge would have known that following her husband's death, Kathryn and her daughter Jocelyn (Joce to her friends) had sold the family home in Santa Clara County and moved east to be nearer her oldest daughter. Had he accessed public records easily available online, he would have known she had recently purchased bottling plants in Michigan and Minnesota. Were he particularly diligent he might have even known that the Banks, man and wife, had been especially generous to Republican candidates at both the state and national level, had contributed lavishly (and unsuccessfully) to California Proposition 8, and twice been guests of the Koch brothers at their strategy sessions at the Esmerelda Renaissance Resort just outside Palm Springs.

"Mrs. Banks," he might have said, hand extended. "What a pleasure."

They made small talk on the courtyard—she'd seen the theater coming in and asked about the summer season: they were staging *Shrek: The Musical*—and then got into Drudge's Tahoe and drove north.

The bottling plant sat thirteen miles out of town, the land ascending, rising from the valley into the rolling hills, everything green, everything alive. What poverty there was—trailers, concrete stoops crowded with washers and dogs—appeared more as authentication than blight. They passed a fledgling vineyard and a fading billboard—HOW DO

YOU LIKE YOUR ETERNITY? SMOKING OR NON?—and parked on a gravel fire road beneath the beech and white pine, ahead of them a gate pulled shut.

"One moment and I'll just…"

But when Drudge went to open the gate Kathryn Banks said she'd rather walk down, see the land, get a sense of things.

"You sure? It's quarter of a mile."

"I don't mind," she said. "A day like this."

They wound uphill through the dense forest, the road overhung with white pine and cut with the runoff of spring rain, but at the switchback it opened onto a long sweep of pasture, the path lined with sunflowers. The building itself appeared in a fold of land, block walls and a metal roof, like an airplane hangar removed to a landscape painting, the Hudson River School gone post-industrial. The bottling plant had closed in March of 2003, a victim, according to bankruptcy filings, of heightened security requirements after 9/11.

"But everything's intact?"

They wound uphill through the dense forest, the road overhung with white pine and cut with the runoff of spring rain…

"Like the day they left it. I've seen it myself."

He was right, of course. The raw tank and the booster pump, the quartz and carbon filters. The winding belts that led from the filling and capping machine on to the shrink-wrap— it was all exactly as it had been left, functional and clean. Cleaner, in fact, as Drudge had hired a service to pressure wash the interior, flushing out the dust and grime and a family of field mice so resilient he'd debated hiring a falconer.

"I'll have to have someone check the condition of the machinery," she said.

"Of course," Drudge said, smiling his bright smile.

"I could get a team down here by, say, middle of the week."

"I can be here at your convenience."

"They'd need to check the transfer pump, a few other things. Is there power?"

"I can certainly get it on."

She stood nodding, bottom lip caught between her teeth.

"It might be useful to find a local partner," she said.

"I can look into that if you like."

"Someone with a good sense of the business climate, local knowledge."

"I can certainly look into that, absolutely."

She turned then, no longer nodding, no longer biting her lip.

She had, it appeared, decided.

"And the price?" she asked.

But she already knew the price. It was the price that had drawn her. 800K. Absurdly cheap, even if the machinery was no longer operational—though she could tell by looking at it that it still was. Her husband had taught her that much at least.

"Let me make a call," she said, and walked out of the cool, dim interior into the warm sun.

It was all, they were both thinking, too good to be true.

And it was, and they knew it.

That was Saturday.

■ ■ ■

Sundays Monty Drudge kept the Sabbath, driving south from Mountain View to Abingdon Baptist, an octagonal arena of sound and light where three thousand parishioners met over coffee and crullers to celebrate the resurrection of both their Lord (via God's grace) and the greater fossil fuel industry (via the grace—and subsidies—of the Trump administration).

Abingdon was the legal hub of the region's coal companies and was littered with lawyers and executives and former legislatures who had retired here in order to drink bourbon at Morgan's while their wives got their mani-pedis at the Martha Washington Inn. You could drive around the countryside in your vintage Aston-Martin thinking about the founding fathers while antiquing for stoneware or another corner cupboard. Monty Drudge made the half-hour drive for reasons economic: the church provided a gateway to his moneyed clientele, and more often than not he stuck around for lamb and roasted potatoes in this or that paneled dining room.

So it was that two weeks after Kathryn Banks's visit he found himself having Sunday dinner in a Main Street bistro with Jeff Morgan. Morgan owned a chain of interstate Bojangles, thirteen restaurants spread north along I-81. He had spent two years as a missionary in Sierra Leone and while he had found salvation, he had lost his wife Carol who left him at the Freetown Radisson to return home and take up with a North Carolina carpenter known to his 8000 followers on Instagram as The Wood Shaver.

"Except he doesn't even build houses or barns or whatever," Jeff said. "It's god-dang 'wood art,' or 'wood sculpture,' which, excuse me, but that's just bullshit is what that is."

The previous week Banks had sent down both a lawyer and a mechanical engineer. The machinery had functioned exactly as it should and now the papers were being drawn up.

When the waitress—Drudge recognized her from one of the local theater productions and made a mental note to stop back by later in the week—brought out a torte for Morgan and a coffee for himself, Drudge switched the conversation to the bottling plant.

"You finally selling that son of a bitch?" Morgan was all chocolatey teeth, powdered sugar in his beard.

"Like you didn't hear?"

"I heard some little old lady from California bought it."

"From Virginia," Drudge corrected, "by way of California. Just to be clear"

Morgan smiled.

"Well, good for you, brother. What's the commission on a deal like that?"

"What are you up to these days, Jeff?"

"Ten percent of what? Seven, eight hundred K?"

"Cause a little bird told me you were spending your days driving up and down the highway bugging the fry cooks."

"A little bird told you that?"

"Checking the sweet tea for sugar. Checking the bathrooms for toilet paper."

"It's called quality control."

"It's called boredom. You really love biscuits that much?"

"I love profit that much," he said. The tines of the fork came out of his mouth gleaming. "How bout that?"

"How bout that indeed. But listen for a minute."

The woman, the California Yankee via Virginia via wherever the hell she hailed from, needed a partner, someone local, someone with area contacts.

"Ah." Morgan had the chocolate smile thing down. "So that's what this was about. She wants how much, a third of the stake, half?"

"She doesn't want any money."

"Don't tell me two-goddamn-thirds."

"Zero. She's buying local knowledge."

"Local knowledge."

"She wants someone onboard who's from here."

"Thus the invitation to lunch." He attempted to wipe the chocolate from his face. "Look, I'm flattered, but I'm not interested."

"I don't believe that."

"I appreciate it, but I'm not. This thing with Carol—"

"Jesus, Jeff."

"This thing with Carol. Seriously. It just sort of took the starch out of me."

"Would a twenty percent stake put it back in you?"

Morgan took his napkin from his lap, inspected it, quartered it, and, finally, draped it over his dessert plate as if it were a fallen comrade.

"Twenty percent?"

"So you're listening?"

"I'm listening."

"Or maybe you just can't get away long enough from all that chicken and biscuits and dirty rice?"

"Goddamn, brother. I said I'm listening."

■ ■ ■

Ownership was transferred on the second of June, 2017, and while Banks LLC. held a controlling interest, a minority stake (twenty-five percent after negotiations) fell to Morgan Enterprises. Two days later Jeff hired a secretary and set up an office on the premises. A week after that, water samples were taken from Morgan's kitchen sink and shipped to Richmond for testing. This wasn't so much obfuscation—the water was pure as a Christian's heart—so much as convenience: the pumps would take a few days to get operational and there was no sense in delaying.

Jeff called a friend with Dollar General to see if maybe they were interested in a distribution deal and sure, maybe, we'll see.

Three days later revival began.

■ ■ ■

Revival in the southern church goes back as far as the brush arbor. The circuit-riding preacher arrives via horseback or Edsel or, in the case of Abingdon Baptist, a Land Rover driven south from Arlington, to drive membership and quench a collective thirst for the water of life. While tradition called for a week of prayer and repentance, market forces had compelled the church to consolidate to a single night, that night being Sunday, the eighth of June. The preacher in this case, Dr. Michael Fuzzeli, was not so much a Soul Saver as a political organizer currently on leave from his own church (Baptist, mega) and spending a year as a research fellow at the Heritage Foundation. It was known that Reverend Fuzzeli had the ear of the president, and the presence of such a Beltway heavyweight brought out the area's business and political elite, including, but not limited to, former Congressman (R—Ninth District) Gresham Manley. Manley had served two terms in the

While tradition called for a week of prayer and repentance, market forces had compelled the church to consolidate to a single night...

halls of power but then, more taken with his own electability than the electorate, lost a bid for Governor, polling, alas, in the single digits. There followed a period of soul-searching involving affairs with both a staff intern from UVA (nineteen and perfectly legal) and low-grade benzodiazepines (Oxys, ten milligram Percs—but only occasionally), ultimately culminating in twenty-eight days at the Wildflower Recovery Center and a YouTube confessional where he tearfully apologized for his misdeeds and announced his intention to reenter public life as the Servant-Leader God intended him be.

But God had other ideas, and the night Manley arrived to hear Reverend Fuzzeli deliver his sermon "Gifts of the Spirit," he had put aside all plans of returning to office (the focus groups were less than positive), and accepted a job with the World Food Program. It was a sort of sinecure, he supposed, but a good job, and he was excited, maybe a little scared. He needed comfort. In a week, he'd be in Rome organizing aid efforts in the Sahel, and overcome with a certain sentimentality, had come, he supposed, to say goodbye.

Looking back, Manley would come to believe that winding up thigh-to-thigh in the pew by Jeff Morgan could only be viewed as God's inscrutable will. That they fell into conversation, Manley revealing his imminent departure—"Goddamn, Gresh, Rome?"—could only be seen as, well, a Gift of the Spirit. And then Africa came up.

"Africa?"

"I'll be working in the Sahel. Mali, Niger, Chad—"

"Jesus, man, I know the Sahel. I spent the two best years of my life in Africa, Carol and me. Tell you what, let me buy you a drink."

Manley didn't drink anymore, but he did accept the invitation, so that they wound up at The Tavern on Main, leaning forward over glasses of Woodford and a Diet 7Up, no ice, but yes, a straw, please, plastic, because he was sick of those tree-huggers telling him what to do. Manley had spent the weeks since accepting the position wishing badly for a different life, so when Morgan confessed how jealous he was—"I'd love to be you right now, brother."—Manley was willing to hear it. Eventually, the conversation turned to Morgan, his divorce, his fried chicken, and, a mere afterthought at this point, his water-bottling venture.

"Hey," Manley said, "are you for real?"

"About the water? Completely."

"You know we deliver water to Africa. All over the world, actually."

"I did not know that, my friend."

"At least I think we do. You know?"

"Yeah."

"Hey, if something were to ever come up."

"Sure, yeah," Morgan said, now drunk and unable to imagine anything past those days in Freetown, Carol on the balcony of the Radisson in giant sunglasses and gauzy sarong, "keep me in mind."

■ ■ ■

But the only thing Gresham Manley could keep in mind was how much he hated Rome. It was dirty, it was hot. When he tooled around the Palazzo delle Esposizioni in white Nikes and fanny pack the locals looked like he was some dumb American which, obviously, he so was not. He liked Africa better. He was spending two or three days a week in Niamey or Bamako, flying down on a baby blue Hercules to oversee the distribution of this pallet of grain or that crate of tractor parts. He'd started keeping a blog called "Dispatches from the Dark Continent," then, realizing he was in violation of both departmental policy and good taste, had started simply emailing his reflections to his old friend Jeff Morgan. Though Morgan only responded to every third or fourth post—"Good stuff, buddy!!!"—Manley was grateful for an audience. In his darker moments, Manley refused to entertain the possibility that Morgan was his only friend, and, if you got down to it, not really a friend at all. But Gresham Manley's one true talent was ingratiating himself in places he was otherwise unwelcome, so when he found his department on the verge of opening bidding on a new contract (7.5 million dollars of water to be delivered in one liter bottles for distribution throughout the Sahel) Manley very casually—it involved no more than a single click of his mouse—changed the bidding status from "open" to "closed." Then, in what he would later describe to the Inspector General's Office as a fit of temporary insanity brought on by the heat and a nascent case of (undiagnosed) Typhoid fever, inserted a two in front of the 7.5. 27.5 million dollars the figure became. 27.5 million to be paid for 7.5 millions dollars worth of water.

Then he picked up the phone and, despite the time difference, called Jeff Morgan.

■ ■ ■

In July, Kathryn Banks attended the Spring Cup in Middleburg where both her daughters were participating in the individual dressage (both were said to be horse-crazy, and a look at the Instagram pics of the Dorado riding boots lining their closets like soldiers in a North Korean parade would seem to attest to as much). It was to be a grand day, announcing, as she imagined it, her arrival in Virginia society, a regional trumpeting of her wealth, taste, and gathering influence. It was a classy affair and the last person she wanted in attendance was Jeff Morgan—she had met him twice, both times equally underwhelmed, and since then had given no thought to her new bottling plant. But she had a member's box, so when he asked, repeatedly, insistently, what was she to say but yes, come, of course. He had good news, he said. She supposed that with the grace of God and a sufficient quantity of gin she could handle as much.

The Spring Cup is arguably the oldest horse race in the United States. As such, it holds its attendees to a standard of dress that makes most derbies appear as receptions at the local Hampton Inn, all Business Casual and a party tray from Chick-fil-A. But here, the landed gentry of Old Virginia dressed in seersuckers by Thom Browne and sun hats by Etro while rubbing well-moisturized elbows with the Beltway elite, the retired three-stars, the lobbyists, the blonde with the high cheekbones and a spot on Fox & Friends. It was not so much the world Kathryn Banks preferred so much as the one only one she acknowledged.

So when she saw Jeff Morgan coming through the crowd in khakis and a golf shirt that read—good Lord—18th Annual Bob Evans Charity Golf Classic, she felt herself go brittle, a sharpening of her already sharp features. She met him down by the infield fence, away from anyone she might recognize, and exhaled with great deliberateness. She would give him two minutes.

"I just saw a man in a pink suit," he said.

"How lovely."

"Had the sort of frilly collar if you know what I'm talking about."

But here, the landed gentry of Old Virginia dressed in seersuckers by Thom Browne and sun hats by Etro while rubbing well-moisturized elbows with the Beltway elite...

"You'll see those now and then."

"He looked queer to me but I'm bad about those things."

"What exactly did you want to talk about, Mr. Morgan?"

"Like ruffles is what you'd call them. A grown man, I'm talking about."

He held a champagne flute, a single raspberry having sunk to the bottom.

"Business, I presume," Banks said.

He downed the champagne, hesitated, and then ate the raspberry.

"Yes, ma'am," he said. "Business, indeed."

Somehow those two minutes turned into ten, and then twenty, and then Banks was escorting him up to her box, oblivious to the expensive clamor all around her because Morgan had said the magic words. Morgan had said, "Twenty-seven point five mil, ma'am."

"And this man?"

"Gresham Manley."

"This Gresham Manley. He's a friend of yours?"

"So to speak," Morgan said. "I mean yes, so far, I guess, as he has friends."

"Don't we already have a deal to distribute through—where?"

"Dollar General. But this is different," he said. "This is another order of magnitude, profit-wise."

They were leaned against the open window of the box, around them Kathryn's new friends, her daughters friends, around her the world she would shortly come to rule through not so much the heft of her bank account as the force of her will.

"And this is legal?" she asked.

He shrugged. "It's just a contract."

"For 27.5 million."

"I'd say we'd turn 21, 22 mil in straight profit. But the thing is, we'd have to ramp up production."

"What would that entail?"

And with this he took not a business plan from an attaché case but a single sheet of notebook paper from his pocket. On it, he had diagrammed the layout of the RAIN! facility.

"We drill a second well just down the slope here" he said. "Pump the water back up to the bottling facility. Up front costs are maybe two mil but the return—Lord."

"Couldn't we just up production from the primary?"

"Unfortunately no. We couldn't meet the contract demand."

"You're sure of this?"

"You can send your man down if you like, but I've looked at it ten different ways."

"So a second well."

"Yes, ma'am."

"And you can do this?"

"We'd have to it tested, approved, all that legal shit."

"That's nothing."

"Water samples and so on."

"That's a mere formality." She looked out at the track where the horses were being led from the infield tunnel, beside them small men in bright jumpsuits.

"So..." Morgan said.

"So call your so to speak friend back. Sign the papers."

"Yes, ma'am."

"Get that well in the ground."

"Yes, goddamn, ma'am," he said, and slapped the notebook paper against his thigh.

"Oh, and Mr. Morgan," she called to him as he was leaving.

He paused and grinned his big cracker grin.

"Next time," she said, "wear a tie."

■ ■ ■

Phone records indicate Morgan called Gresham Manley that night. It was early morning in Rome and Manley picked up. Two days later, they began to drill the second well just down the slope from the primary borehole. It was three weeks later that Manley called back to let his old pal know that the contract had now made its way through the bureaucratic tangle that was the World Food Program and was ready for a signature.

■ ■ ■

Gresham Manley's call went to voicemail. Not that Jeff Morgan was avoiding him. It was more that Morgan suddenly found himself sunk in a mire of his own trouble. RAIN! had pumped its first samples from the second well and, per state regulations, submitted them to the Department of Health and Environmental Control. The A and B samples were bottled and labeled and off to the state office in Richmond. It had happened without his consent—in a fit of initiative his plant manager had sent them, but while Jeff would have preferred submitting samples from the well that pumped cool mountain water into his house, he wasn't worried. It was a formality. They'd be flying water into the Sahel by autumn. But then Morgan got a call from Ben Johnson, a distant relative he now and then ran into at family reunions beneath the picnic shelter at Grayson Highlands State Park, the big shelter, he meant. Morgan was head of Dairy, Soft Drinks, and Bottled Water (this is what was meant by "local knowledge") and called with some very troubling news.

A week after sending the samples, Johnson phoned to say that the water he had just tested contained unusually high levels of dioxins.

"That can't be."

But somewhere far away in an office park Morgan swore it was.

"Jeff, I'm telling you, you've got chlorinated hydrocarbons running out the ying-yang."

"I got what?"

"Aldrin, dieldrin, DDT—"

"DDT's banned, I thought."

"It is. But these things have hell of a half-life, cuz. Where'd you bottle this again?"

"North of Mountain View," Morgan said. "In a goddamn pristine place. You can see the info there on the form. This absolutely can't be."

"I don't know what to say except sorry."

"Did you check the B sample?"

"The results are right here in front of me."

"But we checked out before. What the hell?"

"But that was a different well."

"Like two-hundred meters up the slope."

"Up the slope you say?"

"Yes, up the goddamn slope, where else?

"Well, I'm guessing you've got run-off, cuz."

"Bullshit we've got runoff. We've got reverse osmosis is what we've got. We've got carbon filtration. I watched a fucking Wiki-How probably eighteen times. Hired some hydrologist out of fucking Atlanta."

"But did you look at your soil mobility?"

"My what?"

A week after sending the samples, Johnson phoned to say that the water he had just tested contained unusually high levels of dioxins.

"Your soil—"

"Look. Just sit tight. I'm driving up there."

"To Richmond?"

"Has anyone else seen this?"

"Just the lab tech, but there's no identifying info on it, so—"

"All right. That's good. Look, just sit tight and don't do anything till I get there."

"You really driving up?"

"Don't call anyone."

"I gotcha."

"Don't even look at anyone. I'm fucking serious, Ben."

"I gotcha. Relax."

But there was no relaxing. What there was, was Jeff Morgan making the five hour drive in four so that it was early afternoon when he sat on the brushed steel counter of the lab that adjoined Ben Morgan's office, report in one hand, his bursting head in the other.

"So I did some research," Johnson said, and raised an open palm when his cousin looked up in panic. "Didn't talk to anybody, don't worry. But I looked up the file on your bottling plant. Take a look here." He handed Morgan a sheaf of pages, dot-matrix printed down the center, three-hole punched in the corner.

"Why did you tell me they closed?" Johnson asked. "Back in 2002."

"I never said. But it was security costs after 9/11."

Johnson tapped the sheets Morgan held.

"I think you better read that."

He did, the sinking sensation quickly giving way to nausea. "Pesticides?"

"Like I said, running out the ying-yang."

"How the fuck did they hide this?"

"Did you ask for the papers?"

"I don't know."

"This is all public record," Johnson said with a shrug. "I had to know where to look, but it's all out there. I guess no one bothered to track it down? Or maybe no one cared?"

Either way, the papers revealed that while the bottling plant did indeed cite security costs as the reason for declaring bankruptcy, they had failed to mention that water tests conducted in December 2001 had revealed the same elevated levels of chlorinated hydrocarbons that were now showing up in Well 2 and likely would have been found in Well 1 had that sample not come from Morgan's kitchen sink.

"I'm guessing once the water tested dirty they went and closed preemptively," Johnson said. "Avoid potential lawsuits, keep regulators out."

"You mean people like you?"

Johnson shrugged.

"They probably tested it in-house. By law they had to release the result, but since they had already closed it just slipped into the public record."

"You found it."

Again, Johnson gave a shrug.

"Yeah, but I knew where to look."

"And it's still there," Morgan asked, "in the water?"

"Half-life. It just takes forever for that shit to go away."

"But there's nothing up there. Trees and grass and blue sky. I just don't…"

"Read the bottom."

Morgan did.

"An apple orchard," he said.

"I'm guessing they sprayed pretty heavy back in the day," Johnson said. "Pesticides, you know? That stuffs seeps, cuz."

"Run-off."

"I'd say you got lucky with the first well. In fact, I'm betting if we tested it again you'd get some elevated number there too. In fact, I'm betting what you supplied was maybe not what you labeled, were they, Jeff?"

"Jesus."

"Were they?"

Morgan nodded his heavy head. What had been a low thrum behind his eyes had been replaced with the buzz of action. What was 25% of 27.5 million? He had 6.875 million reasons to do something.

"Can I take these?" he asked about the papers.

"Sure," Johnson said. "I just printed them off the internet."

"This report too?"

"Well—"

He went for the two water samples so quick Johnson found himself jumping back. Morgan was hunched forward, papers and bottles clutched to his chest. But even hunched forward he was a big man.

"Actually, Jeff, the water I can't let you take—"

"I'll be in touch, all right?"

"The samples are kind of state property now."

"I'm sorry," Morgan said. "I'll be in touch."

"Jeff?"

Morgan made it as far as the door before he stopped and walked back over. But something had changed. He stood upright now and his eyes had acquired a clarity that would have frightened Johnson had he not known that—actually, he was flat-out scared.

"Not a word about this, all right?" Morgan said. "These samples never happened. You understand?"

Johnson made his body as still as possible.

"Nod if you understand?"

Johnson made his head nod. If it was slight, it was also all he managed.

■ ■ ■

That night, Morgan's phone continued to flash, but he sunk deep into gloom and four glasses of Woodford so he didn't bother to listen to the voicemail. So it was the next morning when he heard Gresham Manley sounding particularly tinny and chipper.

"Hey, buddy! I got a contract sitting right here in front of me. I think you're gonna want to give me a call soon as you can."

That afternoon Morgan drove north to visit Kathryn Banks.

■ ■ ■

It was August when Monty Drudge got a call from Jeff Morgan inviting him to lunch. Drudge had been seeing the waitress/actress he'd met months ago with Morgan, and hadn't heard from him since putting together the water deal, as he had come to think of it. But business is a web or a spiral, or some other tacky tangled thing, so when Jeff called asking Monty to join him and his cousin Ben Johnson he wasn't the least surprised.

They met at the Mountain View Country Club and migrated from the zinc bar with its Edison bulbs and dapper barkeeps to one of the tables that overlooked the fairway.

Morgan appeared sunburned but happy.

"Yeah, old Ben here," he said, slapping his sheepish cousin on the back, "had a dear aunt pass away—didn't even know her really, did you, Ben? But here she up and left her entire estate to him. Now he's looking for a nice piece of property down here to retire on. Aren't you, Ben?"

Monty found him a twelve-acre estate with a stream, a saltwater pool, and a long view of green mountains. 642K of which he earned six percent. He took his waitress/actress to South Beach to celebrate. Around the time RAIN!'s first shipment of water was loaded onto pallets and slipped into the belly of a C-141 Starlifter at Pope Air Force Base, Ben Johnson bought a membership to the Country Club and a new Kubota tractor. His wife was reading Yelp reviews, searching for a local landscaper though Ben would have rather done things himself. He thought some manual labor might ease his nerves, now that he'd taken early retirement from the state. Still, he was happy. Periodically, he reminded himself to be happy. There had been some misunderstandings regarding water quality and periodically he reminded himself he was glad to have sorted them out. Everything was fine. It was all market forces and he had the house, the wife, the barn with the gorgeous rafters from which, a year later, he would climb into and, reckoning their construction solid enough, tie off the garden hose he would use to hang himself. But that was months in the future. That day, he just needed someone who knew his flowers and shrubs.

■ ■ ■

Meanwhile, Jeff Morgan had dug his passport out of the drawer—the very act dredged up painful memories of Carol—strapped into a jumpseat on the plane, put on a pair of noise-canceling headphones and swallowed an Ambien. A few hours later he watched the cargo door ease open onto the searing brightness of Ouagadougou Airport and the silhouette of his old friend and new business partner, Gresham Manley.

"Hey, buddy!" Manley called into the hulking interior of the plane. He slapped a pallet of shrink-wrapped water and laughed. "Are you thirsty?" ■

UNTITLED 3 (TANNA)

At the block party, everyone knows everyone's grandma. Everyone's got that one auntie with the knock off Chanel. You know, the one that probably slept with her best friend's husband before they were married. Round here, secrets hold good flavor that way. And there might be enough joy here to drain a whole city purple. A cast of deep brown eyes learning how to glitter. I tell you, each house can roll out enough ribs to wrap around the entire neighborhood. Like everyone's daddy pulled one out they chest and slapped barbecue sauce on it. We giving that way. The way a church knows how to hug a note out a baby. The block, a place no matter the black you spit out your gums, you're always home. The home of the dice game. Home of the fresh mac and cheese baked into the gut of the oven. Home of hymn. Home of the before the streetlights come on. Home of the family you can reach and the ones you can't. The ones we still turn dirt over for. The ones that made us make this a place we can call ours.

JASON B. CRAWFORD

GHOULS

See, Quan was what most would call a ghost. He could move in and out of convenience stores undetected and haunted most companies bottom lines. I remember watching him summon two boxes of Mike and Ikes, three bags of hot fries, and a Brisk (the big one) and thinking, *what campfire story is this where my friend is so good at stealing the souls of these aisles?* It's not ideal being friends with a ghost. Sometimes they're there, sometimes they disappear. But in all instances they are dead. See, the spirits caught up with Quan and he had to pay for all the shit he haunted. Cops found him up on 5th after a call in on an armed robbery. Doesn't matter he ain't steal nothing that day, Quan record long enough for the seance to take his bones too. A life for a life, soul for a ghoul.

JASON B. CRAWFORD

ELEPHANT IN THE
BURNING DRESS

There is no god for the gay unfortunates
The abomination stuffed in the black dress, chosen because
the frills hug everything a father could not
or chose not to
Fathers burdened with being the talk of the holiday party
Blessed with the son carrying a lisp
To be the hollow flame lit under the dull pilot burning
down the entire room
Hair still soaked from the gasoline piss of the last man-
made/father-made/lover-made sin
Binged drunk on sweat
Secret letter stitched in between the lip
A man's hand learning to unbraid the seams
And say here I am
Still skeleton in a corset laced to the gums
Are you proud yet? Do you love me?
Inked to the back of the tongue
My full parade dancing off my hands
Ivory dripping from the crevices of the fingers
Carcasses of an outdated text left in the motel covered in
spit and semen
And I just remember assigning a new god to every part of
his body
nothing being more divine than that
And maybe I lost a father in between those sheets
Or maybe I'm just used to being a flame they load with
wood

JASON B. CRAWFORD

ORCHARD

to the man who told me he was tired of hearing about
Strange Fruit

watch them hang // blood oranges // ripened from the
inside out // swollen from the intake of rain // juicy // best
picked when dead // sliced from the tree // cut open
//watch the juices pour out // this field is full of trees //
tombstones // this orchard is a graveyard // watch the vines
wrap around slowly // gripping grapes // this wine has a
bitter aftertaste // hold still and listen to my blackberries
sing a flirtatious tune // it's ripe enough // georgia peaches
still hang // blackening in the sun // this field is full of
tombstones // hanging trees // that bare fruit no one will
eat // like wine blood has a bitter aftertaste // this
graveyard is an orchard of strange bodies

JASON B. CRAWFORD

KEATS
IN YOUR TIME
OF PANDEMIC

KATHLEEN DRISKELL

You remember in Rome you stood in front of a facsimile of a remarkably narrow sleigh bed, a suggestion of the actual bed in which Keats died from consumption when he was twenty-five. What caught your attention were the ceiling carvings over the bed, and you studied them a long while, fascinated by the idea you were looking at one of the last things Keats had seen before dying.

Each square held a carving, a relief of an articulated petaled blossom, a little dome in the center, a pattern repeated again and again, creating a grid. You felt its *fine excess*.

You're a poet, that's what brought you to Keats's bedside. Now, quarantined at home, isolation your best weapon against the Covid-19 pandemic sweeping across America, you remember walking through the muggy crowded streets in Rome toward the museum next to the Spanish Steps. In your quarantine, you are exhausted by the rage you feel at the utter failure of your government. You want a plan. You want action. You want accountability.

You don't want to keep coming back to Keats. You don't want to scuffle again with what the young genius called "negative capability." But what he's written keeps surfacing as if it's your Serenity Prayer: "God give me the grace to 'live with uncertainties, mysteries, doubts without any irritable reaching after fact and reason.'" He's calling for you to live fully within this liminal space, this place of half-knowledge.

The trouble is that Keats's concept of negative capability is slippery. Each time you believe you can hold onto it, it mutates and becomes something else. Then it dissipates before you. It floats away like something *writ* on water.

Nevertheless, it's a beautiful thing. An aesthetic philosophy that dodges and ducks and ultimately throws a knock-out punch to anyone trying to reason out its mysteries. Still you take the punch and get back up. You believe if you could understand more fully what Keats meant by negative capability, you would know how to be here, but also there, and all places in between. You would understand how to keep writing. You want to do as he says, to "let the mind be a thoroughfare for all thoughts," open yourself freely to move among associations. But America's pandemic has made a swamp of your mind.

You brought some students with you to the museum. They milled around the rooms, placing their palms on the glass display tables, leaning in to read archival yellowed manuscripts of letters and old books splayed open, revealing Keats's poems on their brittle pages, while you continued to study the carved ceiling. You've somehow always known, even as a child, that the harvest of pattern is surprise. A gift bestowed by turning away from what's expected. You wonder had Keats lived another year what further would his mind have reaped? Would he have explained negative capability more fully? You wonder if Americans live through this pandemic, who will we be on the other side? How many will be on the other side? What will we understand that we hadn't before?

The rooms upstairs in the Keats museum are dark but for a ray of glaring sunshine streaming through a window. When you glance back at your students they are shadows surrounded by golden motes in the air around them. You think, well, that's *romantic.*

■ ■ ■

You have recently entered the demographic who have a higher risk of dying from Covid-19. You reassure yourself that it won't come for you, not because you're in tip-top shape, but because you have only very slightly crept over the margin of that age group. Mostly you stay inside, wash your hands, work remotely, wear a mask when on rare occasion you venture out to the grocery or slip back to campus to pick up something you need to plan your hybrid courses for the fall. Covid-19 only slightly ups your thinking about mortality—which is to say you often think about mortality.

You assume most would attribute your "flood subject," to the fact you've lived next to a small graveyard for over twenty-five years. They wouldn't know, though, that you are taken most with the oldest grave, that of tiny Alpha Beta Blankenbaker, *Infant*, buried in 1854, the grave closest to you as you fetch the mail at the road. This means the home you live in, which used to be a modest Lutheran church, on the far end of the county where Louisville sits, was built as a complement to the graveyard before the American Civil War, or at least you think that's what it means.

Keats's grave in the Protestant cemetery in Rome is not engraved with his name. His friends asked the stonecutter to carve these words on his marker:

> *This grave contains all that was Mortal of a Young English Poet Who on his Death Bed, in the Bitterness of his Heart at the Malicious Power of his Enemies Desired these Words to be engraven on his Tomb Stone: Here lies One Whose Name was writ in Water.*

Despite his unmarked grave, Keats lives on but for all you know you're the only mortal link to Alpha Beta Blankenbaker—and to her aggrieved parents who laid her to rest more than one hundred years before you were born.

Recently, you've scanned the headstones for death dates between the fall and winter of 1918-1919, wondering if any one next door died from the Spanish Flu epidemic which began with a local outbreak among soldiers at nearby Camp Zachary Taylor. Then, the virus raged for months and infected nearly 70,000 around Louisville, killing at least 2,000. Kentucky's governor Andy Beshear announced yesterday our confirmed Covid-19 infections hit 32,298. 804 Kentuckians have died. Thus far. You don't know why you are trying to make a connection to another historic pandemic, another time. What in the world could it tell you about your own?

You miss your grown children, having them home for long family dinners. They both live in Lexington, an hour away, just far enough so that you have the luxury of missing them while also knowing they can visit often. If you're lucky, around ten p.m. while still at your table, they will stretch and yawn, and announce they are too tired to drive. You watch them climb the stairs with their beloveds, then hear the doors close behind them in their childhood bedrooms. The next morning, you make coffee for them all and listen to the chatter in the kitchen as your husband cooks breakfast. You hear the toast cheerfully pop up. Then predictably when everyone's thoughts turn forward, instead of backwards, you wave from the door as they back out of the driveway.

You realize in a few days it will be your daughter's twenty-fifth birthday. You begin to make plans to celebrate,

You don't know why you are trying to make a connection to another historic pandemic, another time. What in the world could it tell you about your own?

try to imagine how you can all safely come together, but then remember your son has just had a weekend away fishing and kayaking with the boys and so the dinner plans are put on pause until he has time to quarantine.

Keats, his mother Frances, his brother Tom, all died of tuberculosis, which is also a contagious disease spread via small droplets flung through the air by coughing and sneezing. You think, though, that people seem to live longer with tuberculosis than Covid-19, Keats having first coughed up blood in the summer of 1818 after weeks of strenuous hiking with his friend Charles Armitage Brown through the Lake Country and up into Scotland where they ultimately aimed to visit the Hebrides. Keats died February 23, 1821 in Rome where he'd been sent by his friends so that the harsh English winter didn't kill him.

You adjust your thinking after counting months on your fingers. Now in the fifth month of your pandemic, with no end in sight, you hope twenty-nine months is not such a long time.

You find yourself in the yard, cleaning the border beds and remember the tree that once stood near. How you were not prepared for the heart-cuts that nicked as you walked into the side yard and noticed the vast absence of the Ash towering fifty feet above in sky-space, then, below—the devastation of the fence, splintered, collapsed, heaped upon itself. It felt like lightning struck in the middle of your chest, first the violent strike, then the numbing, the tingling through your body. You know this feeling because one night when you were twelve lightning struck just outside the window of your bedroom, and its charge passed through the glass pane into you. You lay in bed stunned, watching an electric glow outline your body.

The shuddering grayness of it, what was left of the Ash, the fence, was then punctuated brightly by Mylar balloons tethered to a squat marble headstone, wafting back and forth against their mooring in the light August breeze. By the headstone was a coned bouquet of carnival-colored carnations. You glanced farther and saw Mr. U—rummaging around the back of his pickup parked in the little gravel pad at the far end of the graveyard. You waved to him, only to say a quick hello, but he walked toward you.

"It's a mess," you called, as he got closer. You waved your arm down what was once a sturdy barrier of sharp pickets, shattered by the tree surgeon's miscalculation, and then sat down on one of the many four- to five-foot sections of tree trunk filling the side yard like an archipelago.

"Yep. A real shame," he agreed, surveying the loss of a 200-year-old tree to the blight of the Borer Beetle which had devastated nearly every Ash tree in Kentucky. He raised his beer can as if to toast you, which seemed odd given the circumstance, but he said, "I'm here to have a birthday drink with my daughter."

"Oh, I see," you said, as if you did. After a moment, you asked, "How long has she been gone now? J—?"

At the mention of his daughter's name, his face brightened, then fell. "Twenty-twelve," he answered. "And it doesn't get any easier," he added, taking in the look on your face, thinking you were thinking that's a long time.

Five years is a long time, but in fact you were thinking just the opposite. You were thinking how recently it seemed when he, alone, had brought her ashes to the graveyard, how you had been pinning up sheets to dry outside that hot day and watched it all. How he had dug the small hole with a garden trowel, reminding you of the way you had recently planted an Annabelle hydrangea against the fence. And you peered surreptitiously between sheets as he measured the hole against the box of ashes and then, satisfied (though that seems an odd word to use), gently nestled the box into the grave and back-filled the hole with his hands, finally patting it as if his daughter were a small child again, and he were tucking her into a snug bed. And how you thought even with a small grave, there is always dirt left over. A little heap of red clay clods, you thought, as you worked down the clothesline, pinning your clean, damp laundry. You thought of your grandmother's grave on Black Panther Mountain, the family's homeplace in West Virginia, but also your other grandmother's ashes in a box still in your coat closet.

And you were remembering him scooting the small headstone out of the bed of his truck, and then waddling with it across the graveyard, and how you worried about his back, his stance awkward as he wriggled it into place over his daughter's tiny grave.

How he had been, still sitting near her grave, hours later, when you unpinned the sun-dried sheets. You were not thinking it hasn't been a long time. What you were thinking was *I'm glad I'm not you.*

A cable TV show replays video of the mass grave excavated in New York at the height of the city's Covid-19 spike. A crane dangles a white box in the air, about to lower it next to another and another and another. You realize this pattern can only be broken when the box is isolated, understood to hold the remains of one who lived a singular life, was loved, or not loved, singularly.

In 1818, after turning twenty-one, Keats completely abandoned medical school, though he had already finished a successful apprenticeship as an apothecary-surgeon and was performing surgeries on his own. As he shifted to focus solely on a career as a professional poet, he and Brown traveled by horse and coach from London to Liverpool and commenced by rail, then by foot, to the Lake District to visit Wordsworth at his home, Rydal Mount, where the famous poet had moved his family in 1813 and was to live until he died in 1850. The cottage, also now a museum, is nestled in a beautiful landscape, among lakes and waterfalls, surrounded most immediately by the terraced gardens that Wordsworth himself designed. Notwithstanding the green slick of rhododendron, the sweeping ferns, brilliant pink flox and the periwinkle spires of larkspur framing the panoramic view of rugged Lake Windermere, that's a long way to go, traveling miles by foot to knock on the cottage door only to find Wordsworth gone, his daughter informing the two men that he was away electioneering for Lord Lonsdale.

Wordsworth had sold out.

That's slang of your own time but nevertheless a term appropriate to describe how the second coming of Romantic poets, Byron, Shelley, Keats, came to feel about Wordsworth, who had traded in his radical democratic ideals for the job security of tax-collecting for the king. The reputation of Coleridge, Wordsworth's early writing partner, had fared a little better among the younger Romantics the two men had arguably birthed. Coleridge had taken to publishing conservative diatribes in the London papers, but at least it was rumored that Coleridge had finally come completely unglued, was probably lawfully insane. Wordsworth was still in his right mind.

Admittedly, resentment toward the older poet was slower to build in Keats who had been gobsmacked by an earlier personal introduction to Wordsworth in London when both were invited to dine in the home of the historical painter Benjamin Robert Haydon. Though ultimately Keats came to see Wordsworth as egotistical, he was able to separate his feelings about the man from Wordsworth's poetry which he held in highest esteem. Keats had inscribed and sent his first book of poems to Wordsworth, hoping the famous poet would open his door wide in welcome and invite Keats and Brown in for tea and also serve up an endorsement of Keats's poetry. And likely Keats hoped Wordsworth's positive response to his work would buoy the young poet after a less than spectacular reception of his debut by the newspaper critics. (Little did Keats know he would be completely savaged two months later by the critics in the influential *Blackwell's Edinburgh Magazine*, reviews so brutal and personal that Shelley would later claim they had hastened Keats's death.)

Finding Wordsworth gone, the two young men, disappointed, walked away from the home, where on the south side of the yard Wordsworth would later plant a tribute garden memorializing his daughter, Dora, said to be his favorite child, who died of TB in 1847. She was forty-three.

You imagine Wordsworth dragging a shovel out to those nascent gardens each day until he died. A vision very similar to the one planted in your mind after you, folding warm towels in your laundry room, looked out the window to see two men digging a grave for the son of a neighbor hit by a truck after he had stopped at the side of the road to change a tire for a stranger.

Keats and Brown walked across the Scottish border and through the countryside, staying in small cheap lodgings or in the homes of shepherds, smoky with peat fires, when they could find no proper inn. They visited St. Michael's Churchyard in Dumfries and stood before the recently erected neo-classical domed mausoleum for Rabbie Burns, which conflicted mightily with Keats's ideal of Burns as the ploughman farmer poet. Later, Keats and Brown visited the Burns homeplace, a long white thatched cottage in Alloway. One side of the home had housed Burns's family; the other side provided a stable for the farm animals to shelter in winter, but in 1818 when Keats arrived, the cottage had been converted to a tavern. The young men rested a bit at the bar, toasting the ploughman poet with their whiskys, before trekking on.

They walked through small villages, where women pulled back lace curtains to peek at the strangers plodding by. They were an odd sight. Keats wore a comical fur hat and a tartan cloak over his shoulders for warmth. Brown had had a tailor sew a suit for him especially for the walking tour: a matching jacket and trousers in a bright red tartan meant to honor his Scottish heritage. They slogged through muddy meadows which sucked at their leather boots, soaking their socks and withering the pink flesh on their feet, on the way toward and over the mountains and to the sea.

Keats and Brown hired a boat to sail to Staffa of the Inner Hebrides and climbed in the vessel only large enough to hold the pair and the boat's pilot, who deftly maneuvered up and down, bucking over sea swells on the short voyage toward Fingal Cave, a towering, glittering cavern lined on either side by basalt columns, "a cathedral in the sea," Keats called it later in his letters, writing that the water washed in a "lurking gloom of purple." It impressed Keats beyond measure and was precisely the sort of unfamiliar landscape he wanted to

They walked through small villages, where women pulled back lace curtains to peek at the strangers plodding by. They were an odd sight.

experience and write about in an epic poem he had planned to call "Hyperion," which he only had time to partially finish after his trip through Scotland.

It is said that Keats ruined his health—he'd already been suffering from a sore throat which grew more painful with each soggy mile—to climb Ben Nevis, the tallest point in Britain, reputed to afford a vista like no other. Though his companion Brown saw that Keats was visibly weakened and footsore, the pair had been walking, mostly in rain, for nearly six weeks by then, Keats insisted they climb the mountain to take in the spectacular views. Once he summited the rocky cap of Ben Nevis, he couldn't see what he had hoped. A persistent thick mist hung just below the peak and mostly obscured for 360 degrees. His view from the top of Ben Nevis had to be imagined.

On the way down, it was clear to both men then that Keats was too sick to continue with their traveling plans. He and

Brown headed back to London. In August, the worst critical attacks would appear in *Blackwell's*. The critic John Gibson Lockhart, now really only remembered for his cruel review of Keats's poetry, wrote this:

> *We venture to make one small prophecy, that his bookseller will not a second time venture 50 quid upon any thing he can write. It is a better and a wiser thing to be a starved apothecary than a starved poet; so back to the shop Mr John, back to "plasters, pills, and ointment boxes," &c. But, for Heaven's sake, young Sangrado, be a little more sparing of extenuatives and soporifics in your practice than you have been in your poetry.*

That fall, Keats would nurse his younger brother Tom until his death from tuberculosis on the first of December, but just the next spring Keats wrote what are arguably the best odes in the English language: chiefly among them "Ode to a Grecian Urn," "Ode to Autumn," and "Ode to a Nightingale." At least those are your favorites.

Less than a year later young Keats would also be dead, spirited away through purple gloom.

■ ■ ■

Your grandmother had just placed a pot of purple mums on the grave of her old auntie who had died of tuberculosis early in the twentieth century, and then took your hand and led you through the gravestones. You skipped every few steps to keep up, your plaid skirt swishing. You weren't paying attention to anything but her. In her late forties then, your grandmother was still considered a beauty. You'd even heard your mother—who had a prickly relationship with her mother-in-law—admire the way your grandmother had managed to hang on to her looks, to not let herself go. *Always dressed to the nines* your mother would say. Always in stockings, fashionable spectator pumps on her feet. She had on those white shoes with black toes and heels as you walked with her over the lawn of the cemetery. Behind, her heels marked a Morse code of indecipherable dots.

Not realizing what the structure was or how incongruously it sat among the gravestones, you broke free and ran toward it. You put your hands to the glass to better see what was inside, to darken your view. In the dollhouse, the marker taller than you were, a poster-bed with linens. Pillows. Tassels hanging from the curtains at the glass windows. A woven rug of blues and greens on the wooden floor, similar to the braided rug under the dining room table at your grandmother's. You walked around it and around it, your hand trailing the exterior. The peaked shingled roofline twinkled.

It was mysterious.

"The little girl," your grandmother explained—you looked at your grandmother's face trying to comprehend what she was telling you. The bright sky hurt your eyes as you looked up. The little girl died when she was five.

"I'm five," you said.

"Yes, you are," your grandmother said, leaning over, brushing the bangs out of your eyes. "But she died a long time ago during a dreadful pandemic. You are safe and healthy and alive," she said. "And you've been immunized against measles."

You wonder if the dollhouse still stands in the middle of that rural cemetery

Still. That word kicks about in your mouth. A word that both you and Keats are fond of thinking about, of using, and which means, of course, to stay, to remain stopped, to discontinue. But looking into its word-heart we know that definition is only a half-knowledge and rests in tension with its other meaning, which calls us to continue, continue, continue. There's a swift river between you and the other side of this pandemic and the only way to cross, Keats seems to be saying, is to leap from one slick boulder to another, despite being uncertain that you'll make it to the other side. The way he did when sick and sore in Scotland. That's negative capability, you think.

Then, it's all gone.

Again. ■

THE RACE BONE

That old man proclaims, "I don't have a racist bone
in my body."
But where in the body does the race bone lie?

Can we find it on an X-ray?
Is it locked inside the spine?
Does it make its home among the vertebral bones?

Or is it hidden in the femur?
In the ball-and-socket joints of the hip?

Is it in the orbit of bones that surround
the eye?

Does it reside in the ribcage
embedded like a bullet?

Does it lie in wait
beneath the flat bones of the skull?

Where and when does the race bone begin?
Can we trace its origins
in the embryonic skeleton
lighter than a honeybee?
Can we see it in an ultrasound;
or does it begin before fetus, before zygote,
when being is composed of only
the dust of soul?

If we follow our lineage like a creek
to the earliest headstream

could we sweep away the sand and clay
uncover it in the marrow of our history?
Here in our ancestral burying grounds
nothing remains but a mosaic of rain-washed bones
strewn among the stones where once walls stood.
The broken cranium—

> what memories were cradled there?
> What songs?

Is it here
in the spiral of the ear
where the child first discerns
how the word *kindred* contains the whisper of *skin*;
how in the word *brother*
is buried the word *other*?

Here it begins
in the smallest bones of the human body
the stirrup, the anvil, the hammer
where a word vibrates inward
into the labyrinth of the inner ear.

We listen to the world first as children
hear it all singing,
before the razor-wire of speech
slices a distance between us—
where I stand on one side;

> you on the other.

ANSEL ELKINS

ANSEL ELKINS

I wait for her / at the door of the physical world," Ansel Elkins writes in her poem "Ghost at My Door," about a mother whose daughter has disappeared. The whole town is searching, finding only a few traces of the missing girl, but as the months pass by the world—the people occupying it, but also the landscape itself—moves on. Growing, changing, dying, while the mother, observing, remembers. Included in her acclaimed collection *Blue Yodel*, which received the 2014 Yale Series of Younger Poets Prize—and placed her in the storied company of former prize recipients such as James Agee, Adrienne Rich, Carolyn Forché, and Maurice Manning—the poem speaks to the poetic perspective Elkins herself occupies. With her attention to folklore, balladry, dark Romanticism, racism, characters who find themselves othered and disenfranchised, and all manner of haints and obsessions, Elkins explores the beauty and brutality of Southern heritage on the page.

Recently hired as Visiting Assistant Professor in Creative Writing at Berea College, Elkins spoke with *Appalachian Review* editor Jason Kyle Howard about the poetic impulse for her work, navigating teaching during the global pandemic, and how she believes poetry "can offer us nothing and everything" in our present moment.

■ ■ ■

JASON KYLE HOWARD: I remember reading *Blue Yodel* when it came out and thinking *now that's a voice*. Part of what moved me so much was how you write about the intersections of landscape and identity and history and the disenfranchised—"where bloodlines and rivers / are woven together", you write in "Native Memory." How did all of that present itself on the page in the collection?

ANSEL ELKINS: Growing up in Alabama and having family in different parts of the state, I came to see my family and our lives as inextricably tied up with the land. Our family histories and stories were bound to the land; my father was the son of sharecroppers and their years of labor on the land was a connection they were always proud of, and it's what gave them a sense of identity as people who worked hard and were proud people because of that sweat. On my mother's side,

Ansel Elkins *photo: Revell Carr*

the land her family owned (all eight children were given an equal portion of the land) had been a catfish farm during the Depression, and it's where we always gather as a family, and it's where my grandparents are buried. Someone in the family called it Jericho because of the old crumbling stone wall that's on the land. I named my son Jericho to honor our family's connection to this homeplace, and out of a deep sense that our family, no matter the personal pains and losses we've gone through, returns to this place and we're a family. The land is what binds us.

JKH: You and I share a deep interest in engaging with history and archetypes on the page. In *Blue Yodel*, you approach these on a more larger, more famous scale with the poems "The Autobiography of Eve" and "Tennessee Williams on Art and Sex." But you also pay attention to local lore and notoriety, such as gossip and reinvention in "Real Housewives" and the sighting of "Goat Man," who "travels through our country roads on foot" looking like an Old Testament prophet. What attracts you to these themes?

AE: It's so hard to think about why one is attracted to write about the things one writes about. I just feel compelled by certain subjects. Writing about them is a way of me trying to understand them. I'm attracted to radical women who are risk-takers—like Eve and even Clara Bow and Mae West, though they're harder for me to write about—but also people like Goat Man who were legends in Alabama. My father was a photojournalist and knew and photographed Goat Man (I have a portrait of him hanging on my living room wall), and I've always been drawn to people who live on the margins of society. I'm interested in the line between comedy and tragedy, and where one bleeds into the other, and I think reality TV and shows like *Real Housewives* are so wildly popular because we see people performing this caricature of their lives; it becomes grotesque, but we can't look away. Maybe what it comes down to is I'm interested in people—the beautiful and the ugly.

JKH: How did growing up in small town Alabama as a "red Rican"—your uncle's term for a redneck with Puerto Rican ancestry—shape your writing?

AE: Growing up "red Rican," like my uncle Juan calls us, was to grow up on the margins of the white world. We weren't Black, we weren't white, and we didn't know of other Latinx families who lived in our area. We were just...different. We grew up with white privilege, but [we] didn't belong in that world in Alabama. And in small towns, how other people see you (or don't see you) matters. My grandmother's culture shaped our family, and yet I saw much of who she was mocked and dismissed by our white grandfather.

JKH: A thread running through *Blue Yodel* is the need for us to examine and reckon with our history. Do you think that is finally beginning to happen?

AE: If we can't reckon with our history now, I don't know when we will. But a lot of people are intentionally ignorant and looking away. What I feel it comes down to is curiosity about the lives of others. When writing I'm interested in where we can see and access another person's humanity.

JKH: In these times—with over 180,000 dead from Covid-19; with Black Americans being murdered in

the streets and in their homes; with people of color and immigrants facing discrimination; with misogyny, homophobia, and transphobia unleashed—besides being outraged and mobilized to create change, I keep thinking about how much we need the written word. What do you think poetry can offer us right now?

AE: I think poetry can offer us nothing and everything. When it's spoken aloud, in the air, and it's received by another, it can be a bridge that transforms consciousness. I believe poetry's power can be revolutionary—if it is used to disarm people and allow them to listen and feel it. If poetry engages people, it's an imaginative act that they participate in, and that can be incredibly powerful. I believe so many people are in need of poetry who aren't getting it, and the world is a more dangerous place because of that. When poetry engages us imaginatively, it expands our souls.

JKH: Have you been able to write in all the chaos? I've heard different responses from writers of all different stripes—fiction, creative nonfiction, poets, songwriters. Some are unable to write anything, while others have been incredibly productive, finishing drafts and revisions of books.

AE: I have a tornado of a boy who turned three this spring, and for most of the last several months we've been without childcare, so I've been able to write in fits and starts. Fragments of poems. At this moment he is asleep, but I am seated at a child's art table in a tiny chair with my laptop propped up on a dinosaur encyclopedia and [I] look up to see the state of our "fun room"—a training potty covered with dinosaur stickers, Thomas train tracks in a bin, velociraptors and a brachiosaurus and all sorts of tiny plastic ancient lizards and stuffed animals scattered about, and my vodka tonic sweating beside me. In other words, these last few months have been so, so difficult to write. The best times are when I stop beating myself up about what I should be doing and just be in the joy of the present moment and have a naked dance party with my husband and son in the kitchen.

JKH: In addition to your writing, you are also making your mark as a teacher, recently serving for several years as Writer-in-Residence at the University of Kentucky, and now as Visiting Assistant Professor of Writing with an emphasis in poetry here at Berea College. How do you approach your work in the classroom?

AE: As a teacher, I encourage my students to try to free up their imaginations, as Toni Morrison said, and approach writing that way. I also ask them to risk something in their writing, to try to surprise themselves and find where their language is fresh and strange. A lot of it is reading their work aloud, hearing their language in their own voices and taking pride in having created something on the page where before there was nothing.

Writing is an act of discovery, and we have to keep digging by trying different entrances into that writing. My aim as a teacher is for them to tap into their own lyricism and make discoveries of their own lives and the lives of others.

JKH: You're starting here at Berea College in the middle of a global pandemic. That's quite the challenge. How have you been reimagining your courses? How are you talking with your students about our current moment?

AE: This is my first truly online course, and what I'm missing most is just physically being in the same room and having my students read their work aloud. I've tried to recreate some of that intimacy by having one-on-one student conferences so that I feel I can really get to know them and their work on a deeper level.

I give students a different twenty-minute writing exercise every day, in hopes that they will get in the *habit* of writing. I've also asked them to take walks and write about what's right around them, to notice the natural world that surrounds them and try to sharpen their ability to observe and listen and smell and touch the world around them. I've also given them an assignment to just dance by themselves and move around and then write, so that they engage being in the world physically with that part of them that is a writer, instead of just sitting in a chair and typing words on a screen. I've also asked them to write a sketch of Summer 2020 for someone who would read it fifty years from now, someone who has yet to be born. How would they describe their current moment in history? What would be worth remembering?

I am trying to make sense of our current moment too, but I feel I'm walking in the woods at midnight with my hands out in front of me.

JKH: Who are you reading right now? What poetry—or prose—is sustaining you and helping to keep you going?

AE: I just read a poem this week that blew me away: Karisma Price's "My Phone Autocorrects 'Nigga' to 'Night'" in the last issue of *Poetry* magazine. I'm going to search out more of her work. I'm really excited about Ricardo Maldonado's first book, *The Life Assignment*, which is just out and which can't get to my mailbox fast enough. The book I've been returning to again and again this summer is Carlos Drummond de Andrade's selected poems, *Multitudinous Heart*, translated by Richard Zenith:

Ah, let the world exist!
Irreducible to song,
superior to poetry,
roll, world, roll... ∎

HONEY BOY, HONEY BOY

you're a demigod, honey boy:
    a refrain of affirmation

though dulcet still
    you're just human

learn not to rely on sight
    because it's only clear too late, looking back

follow the scent trails your past lives left
    to find the primordial behind your memory

what you need is vision and maybe
    that's how you lost track of questioning

everything, about your creations,
    too busy trying to make a statement

but you are compassionate and clement
    content with your worlding

you empathize with those heavenly bodies
    sewn together by dogma and myth

though where the two meet they typically don't
    mix so you hold them tight with honey, boy

you see it's less tacking more fusing
    honey less saccharine more musing

you're a semi-god, honey boy:
        repeat the spell until it lingers after you've gone

but you really can't afford to wait
        for the magic to happen

things are tough in this economy—
        the words don't come like they used to

there is no speech to describe
        a being without context

nothing for those without
        whose only vocation is language

you put in your morning coffee, to help you
        get through the days that pass too slow

though you know you've got to work
        for your honey, boy

if you want to catch any flies
        now ask yourself

if your poems suffer
        for you or if they simply suffer

you and your buzzing
        your Pandora's box, a swarm

you are more than your chaos, honey boy:
    a chant to bring you calm

so be careful not to drown
    like an insect stuck in your honeyed tongue, boy

it might not be too bad of a storm though,
    people are quite polite about the weather

at most it's inclement, unmerciful
    say it's raining cats and dogs

instead of saying you can't see
    for all the raging in you that you just can't forgive

and the flood is frustration, resentment inundates
    but legends too suffer through the dog days

so pleasure in your skin
    humming like sunset honey

boy have faith in your shining
    and your combs will be full

of the sacrifice you can't yet savor
    yes, you may struggle to wade

through the clingy excess
    of verbiage and ritual so that in the end

of this litany you will believe
    in your sweet invocation

so if you have something to say
　　　say it with honey

boy if there's nothing to say think back
　　　to how that nectar tasted

you are your own worship, honey boy:
　　　recite this when the skies run out of testimony

JOHN Q. MARS

A PEDAGOGICAL LOVE

teach this mulatto / boy what a
shame / Black washed white
to care / for his hair
and you will / teach him how
to take his lover /
from hornets' nest to honored / guest
cradled in kneading / hands needing release / slick
and oiled up / milk-fed and misted / with argan,
vanilla and coconut / consortium of fragrance
and historicity extracted / memories that
manage to free themselves / from the tangle
and waft down /

to give you a clue of / its code
its language / an organ
pulsing as if / breathing an ancestral
instinct / seething to spill over and run / wild-like
his lacquered curls //

ask him: "you ready / to get wavy / baby you know
you can roll / them pearls baby / you know
the magic / already there in the leaves / so full of buzzing
and potential" really they're / spells that supersede / the space
that breaks them / line by line / their integrity unbounded
manifest in his spliffs / smoke grammared
and apostastic /

to split between you: / the Uber back
to Brooklyn / so the banks don't /
break off a piece of the last / cookie
share with him / a kiss

a crowning of / baby hairs just as expressive / (intelligible to you or not) / in a vacuum or a too humid day / —all the sweet things that go round //

JOHN Q. MARS

HOOCHSTROKE

Impulse arrested spills over, and the flood is feeling
the flood is passion, the flood is even madness.
—*Aldous Huxley,* Brave New World

Home is where the heart is   albeit
here the honeysuckle smells so much sweeter.

There's not much to do here   but wait
for the thick   slick sheen of sweat to calcify, so

shut your eyes   tilt back your head.
            Forget

as the amber stream slinks down your throat,
closed up from disuse   feel it burn.

Take big belly breaths to dilute the acid in your eyes.
Blink away the rust   watch the flakes constellate with fireflies

in the dying light.   Don't you worry, now
they won't breach that skyline either.

Have you been grinding your teeth again?
Wake up—   it's still early. Unclench

your jaw and show me those cracked memoirs.
Now crush those stained   milkteeth to fine powder

and just breathe.   Real deep now
            just   like   that.

Savor the agave   dripping from your sinuses.
See how that nectar turns to venom on your tongue?

Remember to exhale through your   mouth.
Now pretend   that wind is enough

to rouse   the neighbor's windchime.
Hear that Hallelujah yayo   deep down in your guts.

Collapse   before you vomit up the copperhead.
       Break

your neck to follow as he slithers by
to claim his throne   upon the baked asphalt.

JOHN Q. MARS

WHERE
HAVE ALL THE
SAFETY PINS GONE?

ANGELA JACKSON-BROWN

2016 was the year of trauma. Prince died. Muhammad Ali died. Harper Lee died. The Pulse nightclub shooting occurred. Philando Castile was murdered by police in front of his girlfriend and her four year-old daughter. Donald Trump was elected president. Trauma. One trauma after another.

My life has seen its fair share of trauma. I was given up for adoption when I was just a few days old. I was suddenly taken away from the foster family that had taken care of me from the time I was surrendered until I was two years old. I was adopted by two parents, but only one of them loved me—my daddy. I was sexually assaulted by an uncle when I was eleven. I was diagnosed with bipolar disorder at twenty-six. I was in a loveless marriage for eleven years. Trauma. One trauma after another.

But the beauty of my life is that I have always found ways to cope with my trauma. Sometimes the coping was in the form of a book like Maya Angelou's *I Know Why The Caged Bird Sings* or Alex Haley's *Roots*. Sometimes the coping was in the form of the stories I wrote as a little girl where I reimagined the parts of my life that brought me pain. When my adopted mother would beat me with a broom handle or a strap, I would pretend that my real mother would come flying in with a fury, slay my adopted dragon, and take me to live in a beautiful castle where little, kinky-haired girls with dark skin would be loved and cherished. Sometimes the coping was in the form of loving mother figures like my Big Mama or my Aunt Lenoria who would pull me close, hug me, and remind me that I was loved, even when I didn't feel that way. Throughout my life, there has always been a talisman that I could reach for that brought me comfort—that told me, *this too shall pass.*

So, after the trauma of the election of 2016, something happened. At first glance, it seemed pretty innocuous. A national "movement" occurred that involved safety pins. Black people, people of color, and marginalized people in general were supposed to see those safety pins on the wearer and interpret the meaning of them to be the following: *This person is an ally. We are safe with them. They will stand up for us in the midst of a racist occurrence. They will advocate for us when we are not in a position to advocate for ourselves.*

I tried to imagine myself taking advantage of this offer of allyship. I tried to imagine a situation when having a white person with one of those pins on their clothing would make me feel safe and supported. Maybe I would be sitting in a public space—maybe a park or an outdoor café—and maybe someone, a white woman or a white man, would demand that I tell them why I was there, and before I could respond, maybe they would reach for their phone to call the police on me for disturbing the peace with my Blackness. But maybe, before they could carry out the call, someone, maybe a another white woman or white man, with a huge, silver, safety pin on their shirt, would walk over and stand between me and the other white person sans the pin, and say, "Not today. Today you will not do this. This woman has done no harm. Go away with your hate." Maybe that would happen. Maybe.

Maybe that pin would operate in the same manner as quilts hanging on a clothes line during slavery, alerting runaway slaves that they indeed had arrived at a house where they could ask, "Friend of Friend?" and feel safe. Just like that safe house during slavery meant the slave could take a breath and know they were protected, maybe that safety pin would do the same for modern day Black folks who didn't always know if someone truly was a "Friend of a Friend." Maybe.

Maybe that pin would become like a symbol of hope that would help to cancel out the vote that took place in 2016, electing a man who openly bragged about grabbing women by their privates. Maybe that pin could undo the damage of "good white folks" voting for someone who bragged that he could "shoot somebody on Fifth Avenue and still not lose any votes." Maybe that pin would change the paradigm and for the first time we would turn a corner and there would be a bright, shiny symbol to alert us all that change really had come. Maybe.

Back in 2016, I posted on social media that I didn't think the "safety pin movement" made any sense whatsoever. And it didn't. To me. I couldn't wrap my brain around it. I thought back to the slavery times when Harriet Tubman would sneak onto various plantations and silently take runaways on the Underground Railroad to freedom. The white allies back then were invisible. They had to be for the allyship to work. They provided their aid under cloak and dagger. They created secret safe spaces within their homes. They didn't announce to the world they were an ally. They just did the work.

Wearing a safety pin and then announcing its meaning to the world seemed counterproductive to me. My thoughts were, if everyone knows about this safety pin, couldn't anyone wear it and mislead someone into believing they were

Wearing a safety pin and then announcing its meaning to the world seemed counterproductive to me.

an ally when they weren't? I asked that question on social media. I was shushed. I responded that the gesture felt more performative than anything else. And then I said I would not feel "safe" assuming just because a person wore a safety pin that they were an ally. Instead of being heard, I was *dragged* by some "allies" who challenged me on every single point I made. Called me ungrateful. Called me shortsighted. Called me everything but a child of God.

One ally *unfriended* me on Facebook because *dammit*, she was trying. And she wished Black people wouldn't make it so hard for white allies to help them. I struggled with my emotions. I struggled to not say too much, fearing I would cause those folks who were on our side to walk away. But it was hard. I had just been told, "If you see me wearing a safety pin, I am someone you can trust." But how could I believe that promise when my words alone were enough for them to attack me? How can you be my ally but not be interested in hearing my thoughts? How can you say, in one breath, *look for me and this pin and you can feel safe, and in another breath you say to me, You ungrateful _____.*

Let me give you the quick rundown on what it means to be an ally for anyone, not just Black folks.

Listen. Period.

Stop trying to run things. I get it—you are used to running things, but if you really want to be an ally, stop thinking you can both be the problem and the solution at the same time.

Stand down.

Trust that Black folks or any group of people who are getting symbolic and literal knees to the neck actually know what they need from allies.

Trust that people who have for generations been pushed outside of the margin understand fully what it will take for them to feel included and seen.

If that is too much for you, it's okay. Maybe your allyship needs to be you cut a check to organizations doing the work. Maybe your support involves you sharing a post on social media. Maybe your solidarity means you talk to your MeMaw and PawPaw about the racist commentary coming out of their mouths during Thanksgiving dinner. Maybe your help involves you registering voters and campaigning for candidates who will serve and protect the most vulnerable members of our society. Maybe your backing is you don't take part in the subjugation of other folks. But what your allyship *shouldn't* be is you telling people what you think they need and arguing with them when they say it isn't. Just know that some of the best allies do their work from behind, not in front.

I have always felt outside of the margin. When I was a little girl, I used to write stories and most times I would only write on the other side of the margin, leaving the space in the middle blank. I remember once daddy asked, "Why are you using so little space? You can write in the middle of the page if you want to."

I said to him, "My words are not good enough to be in the middle of the page yet."

Even as a small child, I didn't believe my words were for such a distinctive place of honor. I understood, even then, that the middle of the page meant belonging and worthiness. And as a Black woman in America, I often feel like I have to continue to prove that I deserve to be inside the margin instead of trying to squeeze myself onto the edges of the page. That little girl who saw her words as being unworthy still lives inside this Black woman, and it doesn't take a lot for her to be reminded of that young girl's feelings of unworthiness. To this day, every story and poem I write begins on the outside of the margin.

I wanted the safety pins to be "a thing." I wanted them to have transformative powers. I wanted to know that I could have a visual that would alert me instantaneously that yes, this person is a friend. This person will go into battle with you. But, sadly, as most performative responses to something as complex as racism and hatred of others go, so went the "safety pin movement." It fizzled out without even a sputter, leaving us, the vulnerable, right back where we started, wondering where have all the safety pins gone?

Fast forward to 2020, and after yet another Black man died at the hands of the police on the streets with a knee to his neck and a young Black woman died after being awakened by armed, plainclothes police, shooting twenty rounds of bullets into her home, I saw something I never saw before in my lifetime. I saw people awaken. I saw allies become true allies. I saw white women and men say, "I will stand between you and the bullet." I saw white women and men question police officers asking, "Why are you detaining this person?" I saw white women and men enter the streets of their community demanding justice *or* no peace.

Yes, I still saw the ugly. I still saw white women and men weaponizing or attempting to weaponize the police in situations where Black people and people of color were doing nothing more than being. I still saw systemic racism in workplaces throughout this country. I still saw poor people get the short end of the stick. I still saw the hatred. I still felt vulnerable. But I also saw hope. ■

THE RIVER

Mother had chosen two names, but when she heard
the thirst in my first cry, she touched her lips to mine
and whispered a third in the language of water.

She knew by then that a name sinks into a body
and becomes a shady bower, a flowering grove, or a mass
grave—and she thought to let me choose. But the choice

does not matter; the same wide river runs through them all,
and though I have given it every name I know, it refuses
to be anything other than river:

river of gray; river of green;
river of gold; river of every season's turn; river where the silent,
silver heron glides over the white bends and every long day;

river where the voiceless, copper trout, who have no name
for themselves, never mistake a fallen petal or fall leaf
for a fly; river where the mayflies rise from their hatch

like glittering, unspoken prayer; river of rest. Come, sit
with me on every bank; we will fill our naked, nameless thirst.
This river is as cool as a new day's morning and never still—

it will lose nothing to our cupped palms and ardent, ready lips.

BENJAMIN CUTLER

ELEGIES OF GATHERING

I
When I first heard the father, I mistook
his lamentation for laughter. How could I—
a boy who had lost nothing, not even his way—
know anything of how
                a heart can crack
against the belly, spill from the mouth, and thicken
the air? I should tell you
                      they sat in the kitchen
and how the mother took my hand—her work-
hardened thumbs against my un-calloused knuckles—
and wet my wrist with her tear-softened cheek.
Don't ever be so stupid, so stupid,
                      don't ever be, she said,
and because I could not stand the sight of grief
mingled with promise, I looked away into the basket-
held silence of her fresh brown eggs—gathered by her
son the morning before we gathered to mourn him.

II
These counted years later, I—a man who has not lost
everything—can think only of the chickens, our three
hens lost in the dusk
                of last summer's storm;
of how the drenched dark kept them from the roost's
dry refuge; of how they did not return in the dawn's
clean light, the light of a rainless day; and of how we baked
the last of their laying into a cake
                      as sweet as forgiveness
and ate it warm with our bare and blameless hands.

III
Did I tell you there were eggs in the kitchen where grief
filled the air like laughter? Did I tell you how grief
and laughter both begin in the belly?

                                       Watch with me, love:
I see a father and a mother the morning after
a night of rain. She takes three eggs—no, two—
in her practiced hands, cracks and whips them well
into a buttered pan. He fries, salts, and serves—
a shared meal from a shared plate.

                                     Did I tell you, love—
yes, I must have—how a belly promises only to empty
and always knows what it needs?

                                     Can you see them, love?
Yes, you must now. They cry (or laugh) as they share
what steams between them. He washes, she dries, they walk
outside—walk together to gather the new day's
eggs in the early morning fog,

                                     enough light to see the love-
worn way through bowing grass, enough to reach into a nest
and feel what is round, warm, and not yet broken.

BENJAMIN CUTLER

SELF-PORTRAIT AS FLY FISHERMAN

He stands still and the creek does not—
a waist-deep shortcut

to nowhere. An arm, bare
to the elbow, nudges the morning

fog. A thread of water-
shine tongues the air. The impossible

reach, his expectant watch.
O to hold in your careful grip

this perilous truth and finesse
its length into a grace: longing

is a long line stretched
and taut in the current—hidden,

wet and waiting. The tug
of a phantom bite. Longing

is the second cast. And the next.
And the next. An arm reaching

beyond reach as long as day-
light allows—

BENJAMIN CUTLER

DEVIL'S WALKING STICK

All souls that sting and gather
against hunger congregate here, and they make
a chorus of their harvest—because what else is there

in the midday heat but this gold
flowering at the crest, this last and solitary blessing
of the year's longest days? Such a late communion—

a high and brimming bounty,
a nectar-rich crown the flightless cannot reach
unwounded. Come, fallen wanderer, take this tree

in your grip; cut it from glory
to walk upon this earth. Why look to Heaven
when the path is root-mapped, underfoot and deeper

still? Every Son of the Morning
knows blooming is brief, that the hike into evening
is long and requires a thorn-bloodied palm. Arrive

and listen, stained staff in hand:
the night is also full of song—each voice a solo
in the cool and flowerless dark, waiting in the dew

for your shadow-sung answer.

BENJAMIN CUTLER

THE
SPRING

SHEILA R. LAMB

That squirrel sat right in the middle of the chicken's feed pan, stuffing his fat cheeks full of corn crumble. Ice and snow pelted down, and then hens were underfoot, eager for their evening meal. Though those birds would peck a mouse to death or quarter a toad—a foursome group effort, each hen heading in its own cardinal direction—they shied away from the squirrels. Used to be I'd let my hound out with the chickens. She'd corner a squirrel quick, catch it by the neck, and shake it until the life was gone. I didn't have a dog anymore—I figured it might outlive me if I got one now—so I made for the manure shovel. I raised it, took aim, and smashed the squirrel, right on the skull. Left it in the pan. Let the hens gather round.

Weather as it was didn't bode well for the squirrels or for anyone who might be driving on the mountain. When you get winter up here, it works something like this: snow and rain stick to the road and then turns into an icy sort of slush. What people don't get when they come up here to hike the trail is the altitude. They don't understand the concept of high-up. They think "country" not "mountain," until they spin out in their underprepared SUV and get caught in the ditch that runs alongside our road. Later, after the storm, Bobby tugs them out in the tow, because ice, altitude, and steep incline don't mix, at least not here on the line between South and Mountain.

The ditch is a waterway, and the spring that fills it begins in my backyard. It's the water for which our entire county is named because somewhere east the spring turns into a river, into a bay, into an ocean, but here it is my backyard spring and its run-off is the reason for precarious driving on our mountain road. Way back, Eric wanted to make the spring a tourist site. Charge them a dollar or two to come and see, but the county supervisors ruled no. Said it would be too much traffic or somesuch, even though it takes some doing to find our road and the section of trail it intersects. Eric wanted to bring the tourists up anyhow.

"You can't get people up here without a sign to it," I argued. "And as soon as you set out that sign, Bobby'll come on up and take it down." In addition to driving the tow truck, Bobby was also a county supervisor. No stopping him making money on the side but it was the rest of us that had to kowtow to his rules.

"Bobby can't stop us from doing what we want on our own property, Sarah."

What *you* want to do, I thought loudly. But I only said, "I think he just did."

"It's our spring. One of a kind. Marked from here to the ocean."

I rolled my eyes and shut my mouth. Eric had been a geologist who also fancied himself some sort of expert in tourism and natural springs. Jacob I could talk to, but not Eric. No point in it. After a quarter century of marriage, I knew that Eric would push to do what he wanted but I wasn't going to give in on the spring. I wasn't going to let him give Bobby Winetree a reason to set foot on our property.

Bobby didn't like us none since we bought the cabin twenty some-odd years ago. I had settled in and taught school local while Eric kept one foot in the outside world. Traveled in and out of airports for his geologist work or his mistress meetings, I supposed. I got me a henhouse, a dog, a truck, and then started the egg business which seemed to please most everyone at the time, including Bobby. Enough people done left our mountain, left the county for city work. Bobby learned to be glad for anyone who stayed. He'd probably approve that tourist spring now, so desperate for money the county was.

So, there it was. Another SUV stuck in the ditch that led my spring water to the Atlantic, to the coast of Ireland— where, after all this, I should have just gone. When those doomed-to-wreck cars made it up the road high enough, their headlights reflected onto my Chevy's passenger mirror, then into my bedroom mirror. A little triangle of light let me know when some tourist was trying to reach the trail on the wrong day.

I put on my boots, gloves, picked up the shovel from where I'd left it in the chicken yard. Snow pellets came down thick. I didn't plan on letting whoever was stuck stay at my house—using the old landline was all. Waited a minute more to see if Bobby's headlights shone through the fog and ice. Sometimes people had the right kind of cell service and could call for the tow themselves.

Bobby didn't show so out I went. Bare poplar branches creaked in the wind. I walked fast. When those branches were shorn off the trees, they plunged into the ground, stakes into the heart of the earth. Other limbs fell at less harmful angles, littering the road and my yard until I collected them all for firewood or the wood chipper.

I shined my flashlight. The driver's side window was part way down. A man gripped the steering wheel. He didn't look like the usual hiker that came up this way, swathed in rag wool and fleece. This man was dressed in all black, black ski jacket, black neoprene gloves, like he had to match his vehicle, except for a red knit hat on his head. Like something his grandmother might have crocheted for him years ago. "You need me to make a call?" I asked.

The man didn't respond. Kept his hands where they were and stared straight ahead. His forehead was bleeding a little. Looked like he had hit the dash when he swerved.

"There's a road up there," he answered finally. "GPS says there's a road."

"There's no road. It's the trail."

The man didn't say anything. Stared ahead and I wondered if he was on some sort of drugs. His pupils seemed to pinprick to black and he didn't move except to tighten his hands on the steering wheel, like he'd fall away if he let go.

"You want me to call the tow truck?" I asked again, but by then I had begun to regret my decision to come out here at all. Most folks who got stuck in this spot were young: hikers, college students, or adventurous families, who were grateful for any offer of a phone. This man, though, was dazed. No emotion. Maybe, I reasoned, it was from where he hit his head.

"No. I'll push it out."

I leaned back, balancing on my shovel. The road had only a scrape of sand beneath the ice, laid down from last week's storm. I glanced behind me to my porchlight, a tiny star.

"Mister, there's no pushing this truck out of this ditch uphill." Being all alone sometimes made me forget when people were off-kilter. He turned to me, face contorted, dried blood along his brow. His glare burned into me, hateful-like. The knit hat slipped down when he turned, red blending with the rust color of his blood.

"I said I'll get it." A low growl, the devil's own voice. "Leave."

Fear hit me then, a deep punch in the pit of my stomach. That sound was from something of the beyond. "All right." I picked up my shovel. Used it for balance as I crossed the ice-pocked gravel. Glanced back to make sure he didn't follow even though I felt his hatefulness cling to me. I'd get to the cabin. Turn out all the lights. Keep the .22 at my side. Even so, I hoped the snow would cover my tracks.

■ ■ ■

Bobby appeared on my doorstep the next morning early, before I had the chance to let the hens out of the coop. He had a way of doing that, always showing up whenever it suited him. After the fight over the tourist spring, he'd come up and check on occasion. Make sure we weren't running it on the sly. I always figured Bobby wanted me off this property so he could run the tourist spring himself. Eric I could leave, and I did a time or two, but not this mountain. It pulled me back, it was in my bones, even though I wasn't born to it. Bobby was and, when it all filtered out, that was the problem between us.

I didn't know what made him hunt me out now.

"You should have called me about that man," said Bobby.

"I did. You didn't answer."

"Did you call the office or my cell?"

"I called. After ten." Sometimes my memory didn't serve and maybe I did call his supervisor office instead of the tow truck. Bobby pulled out his cell phone. Scrolled through a list of calls. Hit a button. Probably the erase button, I thought.

"Sheriff's coming up for an investigation," he said, still looking at his phone.

"What for?"

"That man died."

My insides turned cold. I reached into my sweater pocket to catch hold of a couple of hen feathers I'd put there the night before. Black Australorps provided powerful protection. I'd

My insides turned cold. I reached into my sweater pocket to catch hold of a couple of hen feathers I'd put there the night before.

been working with different things—feathers, stones, and such for some time. I disliked the word magic. For me it was more like *working with what I had.*

"Sheriff Brown will be coming up to talk with you."

"Why me?" Pinched the quill ends till I thought my fingers might bleed.

"Your footprints are frozen into the ice. You can see it, clear as day, you walked out and walked back, with a stick or a shovel or something. Clear as day."

I held tight to those feathers in my pocket. "Why are you telling me this, Bobby?"

"Telling you what the sheriff is going to tell you. You should have called 911, not just the tow truck."

"You know my opinion of the emergency services on this mountain."

Bobby looked away, down to the ice-slick porch, over to the light fixture that I'd filled with quartzite. He puzzled over that for a minute. "Well. That was a sad thing, losing your husband like you did. But what I'm telling you, it looks bad for you Miss Sarah, especially with the gash that man had on his head. Looks real bad."

I should have let that man be. Let him be without the freeze of my footprints or the pitch of my shovel nearby. His glom, his hatefulness, followed me up the road, up the waterway, and to my door because Bobby wouldn't be here otherwise. I kept my hand tight around the feathers and wished Bobby would leave so I could get to the quartzite stored in the lamp.

"You might want to call yourself a lawyer, Miss Sarah."

I smoothed down the feathers in my pocket. "I don't have time for your fool notions Bobby. I'm going inside to count eggs."

■ ■ ■

Sheriff Brown showed up as promised. It was lunch time and he finished up a homemade beef sandwich in my driveway, sitting in the front seat of the county four by four. A dab of horseradish rested on his chin when he knocked on my door. "We need to talk about that man that was stuck up here last night."

"All right." I stood out on the porch with him, just like I did with Bobby a few hours earlier. Standing out in the cold might make this whole thing go quicker.

Sheriff took out his little notebook from his pocket. Fumbled for a pen with his thick gloves. "Why didn't you call 911?"

"I called Bobby twice."

"Your messages were on his office phone."

I cringed, embarrassed. Sheriff kept on though. "You didn't call emergency?" I stared at him and his horseradish chin until he said, "Sorry, Miss Sarah."

"That man was perfectly fine when I saw him. Didn't want any help at all. I didn't break a law, did I?"

"That's what we're trying to find out."

"A car wrecked. I asked if he needed help. Said no. Left a message with Bobby's tow service. Did you question Bobby too?" Then it dawned on me. Maybe Bobby sent the sheriff up here to get his own self out of trouble. "Might do you all some good to get some signage down below. Let folks know it's a dead end up here."

"You know how Bobby and them feel about paying for extra signs."

"That man's phone showed the trail was a through-route over the mountain to the highway."

"You talked to that man?"

"I just told you that I did." How any crime ever got solved in this county was beyond me. Maybe none never did.

"I need your snow boots and your shovel, Miss Sarah."

"My boots? My shovel?"

"This one, right here." He pointed to the one on the porch. "Guessing that's the one you carried out to the road?"

I handed him my hiking boots, which were where I left them by the door. He wrapped them in a plastic bag, then took hold of the shovel. He tied another plastic bag around the head of the shovel. I took my feathers from my pocket and twisted the ends with thread. After Bobby's visit, I hadn't time to get to my supply of quartzite, having to take care of the hens and all. The porch light was still on and the stones gave off a nice sparkle in the lamp.

"What's this?" Sheriff asked. He looked close at the top of the shovel head. "Looks like blood."

I squinted at where he was pointing, through all the plastic. "I killed a squirrel with it this morning."

"A squirrel?"

"It was in the coop. Eating all the hen's feed."

Sheriff didn't say anything. He twisted the plastic tighter. I twisted my twine around the feathers. He reached down to pick up my plastic-wrapped shoe and watched me twining. "What are you doing there, Miss Sarah?"

"Waiting for you to either ask me another question or get off my porch."

Sheriff kept staring. I got the notion that horseradish was frozen to his chin and maybe I ought to mention it to him, but he burst out, "You got yourself a charm there?"

I ran my thumb over the braided twine. "You can call it what you want."

He stood there uncomfortable for a minute or two, my shoes and shovel in each of his hands. Finally, he picked his way off the icy steps, slipped once, and used the shovel for balance, just like I had.

After Sheriff Brown left, I focused on what I was making. Checked my winter supplies. Unplugged the phone. Washed the quartz pure in the backyard spring. Added the stones to the three black feathers—twining stone took some time. Switched from thread to leather to hold the stone in place.

Sheriff Brown tied yellow warning tape around the wreck. A couple of teenagers appeared from their homes to see the goings-on but, after a while, left, and melted into the foliage of the community down below. Once, a state trooper appeared with Bobby, walked around the SUV, then it was towed away, and that was about it. No one came up the mountain to check on me or to talk or to buy eggs. No one did in January usually, so I'm not sure where that expectation came from. I hung the black Australorp feathers and quartzite underneath the porch light. Spent the winter days making more and tying them to bare tree branches.

A few weeks later, Sheriff Brown returned with Bobby dancing behind him, wearing slick city shoes. It was a Wednesday, so I suspected Bobby had a county meeting. Sheriff handed me my shovel. "It was squirrel blood."

"I know."

"Here's your shoes."

Finally, he picked his way off the icy steps, slipped once, and used the shovel for balance, just like I had.

"About time. Too cold to be going out in the chicken yard in plain galoshes."

They stood there on my porch. I wanted to shut the door on them but didn't think it be wise to do that to a sheriff. "Well?" I said finally.

"No one's at fault," Sheriff Brown said finally. Like them two wanted to torture me with the waiting. "It was an accident and that man…well, looked like he had some pills and things he was trying to get to the kids here. Some kind of doctor gone bad." They left, ducking the charms, my protection, as they made their way back to the police four by four. The feathers swayed as they passed, quartz catching light on the snow.

■ ■ ■

Seasons changed and the earth warmed to mud. I cracked open the door. Slid out my step stool. Still in my flannel nightgown, I unscrewed the base of the porch light and reached in for the rest of the quartz I'd collected after the snow melt. My morning ritual. Protection from the glom. The thing from that dead man. Evil looking to attach itself.

In the weak sunlight, an old mint-green Ford pickup approached my yard, the kind someone's daddy buys for them old and lets them fix it up with jacked up wheels and suspension. The bed of the truck was filled with survey equipment—a theodolite, tripods. I knew what it was because I still had Eric's in the basement.

The driver, a young man with a ball cap, jumped out and began to crunch his way up my gravel drive. Paused when he saw the twined feathers and quartz tied among green buds of the poplar branches.

"Help you?" I called. "You want eggs?" I'd collected the morning's laying and had some new pinks and greens in my nightgown pocket.

"We're supposed to map out the start of the river, right here at your spring. County supervisor said we could survey here. Said he talked to you."

I bet he did.

"Didn't know it was anyone's property," the young man continued. "Got a permit to survey county land between the road and the trail." He glanced back to his truck to where his two friends waited, a young woman in the middle, another ball-capped boy on the passenger side. Must be some college project they were trying to do here.

Didn't feel like answering them. Not quite yet. Bobby and that damn spring. And Eric too. I cursed him wherever he might be. I set out my workings on the porch rail, like I did every morning. Quartz, feather, egg. A pattern of the three along both porch rails and the front step.

The girl poked her head out the driver's side of the truck window. "Carl, come on."

"Supervisor made a mistake," his other friend called from the passenger side. "Let's go."

Carl looked to the crystal-laden trees. To the feather and eggs on the porch. To me.

"It's protection," I tried to explain. Something he saw, thought he saw, made him run back to his truck and jump in quick. He drove out in reverse, spraying gravel.

"For you." I finished quietly, wondering if this is how it would be. "To keep it from you." ∎

CAROLINA PARAKEET

What I must know is this: why
haven't you yet written the elegy

of the Carolina Parakeet? You
who call winged spirits words,

whose cells ache with each note
lost. You who dream of healing

the broken bones of a South still
on her knees; you who hum

the melody of flitting shadows
drifting across your page.

Perhaps you've scrawled
the piece and shut it

in some drawer with a useless key-
hole, or folded it between pages

of a book you can no longer bear
to open. Yesterday, I knew you

wrote the bird so well her ghost
lifted from your pen, flew through

your bedroom window and into
the wood, where she hovered

until she found her mate. Lacking
your answer, or rather, lacking

a means to ask you the question,
I will do this: close my eyes. Watch

the yellow-green flock swell up
over our mountains until I can't

begin to name their number. Then,
right hand clutching perfect pen,

I will open to a new-blank page,
swallow a lungful of extinction,

and write the poem myself.

EMRY TRANTHAM

LAKESIDE

Look upon a wind-worn water,
its smooth light stubbled
by summer storm—

you have lost the trees, the sky,
the pale eye of the sun
to quiver and wave,

flummox and flow,
and become drowsy
in the new tumult of surface.

To be drawn to the downy
dodge of peak, dip, peak
is to rest until

the weather rests,
which it will.
The wind will lay. Rings

of ripple will surrender
in stretch; the sun will open
to glint the liquid mica,

gone still, clear, mirrored
enough to give you back
a truth you meant

to sink forever in the depths.
And what now?
You may choose

to leap, to leave—
to fall to your knees
and pray for rain.

EMRY TRANTHAM

THE WHITE MOTH

She is in repose when I find her,
white wings stretched against

> the wet concrete of the road.
> I pick her up and hope for a

moment—I might detect a lift
of wing or curl of antenna,

> but the moth is still. On one
> finger I lift her to my eyes, work

over the fuzz of her body
with my gaze, and within three

> of my own heartbeats, declare
> her dead. I won't know the cause

of death—she looks intact, bridal
white and lovely. I lower her near

> my lips and exhale, as if to remind
> her what wings do with wind.

I can't return life to frail limbs.
What does one do with a piece

> of perfect death? I carry her inside
> and close her in a jar.

EMRY TRANTHAM

TOUCH ME NOT

I can't help but rebel
against such spindly demand,
though I suspect there's more
to my affection than contrariness.
Take, for example, the orange buds,
sparked fires pulling my pulse to their warmth,
or the curling green limbs filling
all the space I ask of them. But the pods—
oh, the pods—growing full as summer lingers,
begging me to pinch them
between forefinger and thumb, to squeeze
ever so lightly until they burst
against my palm, seeds spun to the shade
of the forest floor. Perhaps it's the way
that in every language I love,
the thick green beckons—touch me.

EMRY TRANTHAM

THIS PRESENT ABSENCE:
THE GENERATIVE POWER OF EPISTOLARY FORM

JESSIE VAN EERDEN

I sit down to write a letter so I can hear another person listening. So I can be changed into myself. I can say: it is prematurely spring here in February, and I join my present to yours—the present of my writing to the present of your reading, which I must imagine. The letter is a physical trace of me, but it is also my self disembodied; it bears the *press* of our bodies, their youth and their age, as I write and as you open the envelope at your desk and the dog nuzzles to go out and you pause at page three and will come back to it soon.

In this time in our history, of pandemic quarantine and great social division, letters are one way to hold others close. Yet the closeness we feel from a letter is wonderfully strange, since it is a nearness predicated on distance. The addressee is pulsingly present in her absence. For me, letters can generate thoughts which have been inchoate until I suddenly have a specific audience for whom to focus them. As language in a letter invokes its audience, the Other gives shape to the self's interior. In this invocation, there's a disruption of the Other into the sovereign self, and this disruption seems to me the dynamic heart of the epistle, and of literature that takes on epistolary form.

I began researching the form when I was writing my epistolary novel *Call It Horses* (forthcoming from Dzanc Books in March 2021). In early drafts, the novel's straightforward first-person seemed at once unwieldy and lethargic—to whom was my narrator Frankie speaking and why? Suddenly, I had her writing a letter in her dollar-store notebook to Ruth, her aunt's lover who is a linguist, and the voice calibrated itself; the narrator's project became urgent with *the need to tell and reckon with*. All epistles are provoked and present an evident need, so one gift of this form is immediate purpose and urgency.

The umbrella of epistolary literature technically includes any work written as a series of documents, or one that integrates documents, such as letters, diary entries, newspaper clippings, legal files, Facebook posts, tweets. In this essay, though, I will limit our document-focus to the root word of the genre, the *epistle*, the letter. With a few exceptions, we write to people who are absent from us, often because we long for them in some way; thus, when literature adopts the letter form, longing is on display and absence becomes a narrative force. Wonderful polarities are at play—between the said and the unsaid, distance and intimacy, the reader's experience as confidant and that of eavesdropper, the veracity we attribute to a document and the unreliability of letters that lie. The potential for energy, urgency, and narrative pressure is enormous.

Three works have especially illuminated for me the generative power of the epistolary frame: the unread letters in Alice Walker's novel *The Color Purple*, the letter of occasion in Jane McCafferty's story "Thank You for the Music," and the "found letters" of competing truths in Alice Munro's story "A Wilderness Station."

Alice Walker's beloved novel *The Color Purple* is composed of diaristic letters to God written by Celie, a bereft and abused African-American child bride in the South; later in the book, she addresses her letters to her sister Nettie, a missionary to Africa for whom Celie has no address. Nettie's letters to Celie are eventually included as well, though Nettie assumes the letters will go unread because of Celie's oppressive husband, who does indeed hide them. Thus, the novel is a sheaf of letters written without hope of response or connection; as such, the novel's letters are more like journal entries documenting Celie's yearning for a self in the midst of trauma, her attempts to reconcile a fractured life, and both sisters' insuppressible *need to tell*. But the unresponsive addressee is palpably present in the letters, lending a more specific and focused intimacy than a journal entry.[1] Heather Stanfill writes in her essay "An Epistolary Plea," "The letters contain things that the character...can tell to no one even when she has a desperate desire to confide in someone. It isn't just the succession of terrible and wonderful events that happen to each sister that make the story compelling, but their need to express to each other their life stories, even if they believe the stories will never be read."[2] The frame of the unread letter gives us writers rich opportunities to distill and shape a narrative of self-discovery, particularly in a context, like Celie's, that has otherwise silenced a character.

We do assume receipt of the letter in Jane McCafferty's short story "Thank You for the Music," which is a letter of occasion sent to a specific mailing address, the occasion being that the narrator Francine has received a mixed tape through the mail from her old friend Leonarda from whom she has been estranged, and Francine, an agoraphobic whom the mixed tape has empowered to leave her house, is writing to thank her friend: "Each song on your tape has become for me a shelter."[3] The narrative basically follows what happened when she received the tape and how it affected her, progressing song by song on the tape. But the thank-you note frame is also a scaffolding with which to build the history of their friendship that began after teenaged Francine gave up her child for adoption.

Such a story offers readymade intimacy, but the challenge for the writer is to provide the reader with backstory without burdening the letter—addressed to someone familiar with that backstory—with information that stretches realism too far. "With the epistolary mode," writes Bayard Godsave in "Other Epistolaries: When the Fictive Appropriates the Nonfictive Form," "so much depends on what is outside, a world that is merely gestured at, and what we often must construct ourselves."[4] McCafferty skillfully gives a textured feel to the thicketed history of friends smoking on a water tower and listening to a transistor radio, which activates the reader to fill in the gaps. The story is overheard, suggestive; the women's

1   Alice Walker, *The Color Purple* (New York: Harcourt, 1982).
2   Heather Stanfill, "An Epistolary Plea", *The Writer's Chronicle*, September 2012, 102.
3   Jane McCafferty, "Thank You for the Music", *Witness*, Vol. 18, No. 1, 2004, 60.
4   Bayard Godsave, "Other Epistolaries: When the Fictive Appropriates the Nonfictive Form", *The Writer's Chronicle*, March/April 2018, 81.

shared experiences are scenically detailed as news for the reader disguised as reminders for the addressee: "I remember how you stood in the middle of that narrow city street offering me a cigarette you'd rolled yourself, saying, 'It's European.'" But the letter also supplies information that's new to Leonarda, with a tone of confession: "I love you, I wanted to say then," the real subject of the letter.[5] The narrative stays within the conventions of the occasion of the thank-you note while also energetically overspilling those conventions.

Things get even more thicketed when a story has multiple letter-writers, multiple recipients, and truth that doesn't add up, as we have in the "found correspondence" of Alice Munro's story "A Wilderness Station." This polyvocal story is made up of letters, as well as other types of written accounts, spanning from 1852 to 1959. The writers include a matron of an orphanage; two brothers, Simon and George Herron, striking out on the Canadian frontier, one of whom mail-orders a bride; a clerk of the peace; a minister; the mail-ordered bride herself, Annie Herron, turned inmate; and the granddaughter of the clerk of the peace.[6] Like Walker's and McCafferty's narratives, this story is also "pure-oxygen" epistle, with no narration contextualizing the documents.

At the center of the story lies the mysterious death of Simon, one of the brothers, Annie's husband—accident or murder, and if murder, then by whose hand? The story beautifully illustrates how epistolary literature can center on silences and secrets, on both intimate revelation and deliberate subterfuge. The reader acts as sleuth as the constantly revised, nonlinear narrative unravels by way of the correspondence carefully sequenced by Munro; the reader, like a person going through a box of records in a courthouse, must decide whom to believe. This polyvocality can be generative when we have a narrative of mystery and disputed truth.

Bayard Godsave writes that "the goal of traditional realism, many have claimed, is to make the reader forget they are reading." But he notes, quoting Linda Kauffman's critical text *Special Delivery*, that "epistolary texts 'always lead us back to their writing.'"[7] They keep readers aware of the letter as artifact, of the addressee as a present, acitve force within the narrative. Epistolary literature, ultimately, offers writers and readers a way to explore the invention of truth.

■ ■ ■

Writing Prompts

Write a story in the form of a thank-you note, or other occasional correspondence (condolence, congratulations, complaint to a manufacturer about a product, fan letter). Another model for this exercise is Amy Hempel's story "Reference #388475848-5," written as a letter that disputes a parking ticket, found in *Fakes: An Anthology of Pseudo-Interviews, Faux-Lectures, Quasi-Letters, "Found" Texts, and Other Fraudulent Artifacts,* Eds. Shields & Vollmer.

If you're working on a story with a central shadowy event, like the murder in "A Wilderness Station," break out the narrative as letters written by a few different characters, lending the story a feel of a "found correspondence" and allowing for polyvocality. Note how a letter's audience determines tone, motivation, gaps, narrative choices, level of truthfulness.

Linda Kauffman, in *Special Delivery*, writes that epistolary literature "nurtures the illusion of speaking with the one

5   McCafferty, 63.
6   Alice Munro, "A Wilderness Station", *Selected Stories* (New York: Vintage, 1997), 604-33.
7   Godsave, 80.

whose absence is intolerable" (xix). Write a piece addressed to a person whose absence is most intolerable for you (or for your character). You might choose a narrative frame like Walker's that has the letter go unread.

Many of us love to read compendiums of correspondence—maybe you've dipped into the letters of Vincent van Gogh, or of Flannery O'Connor in *The Habit of Being*, or your favorite artist or family members. If there is a compendium that means a lot to you, try either or both of these prompts:

- Create a poem of "found text" pulled from the letters and arranged according to your purpose.
- Write in persona using the letter-voice you've "heard" within the actual correspondence. (Jessica Jacobs's *Pelvis with Distance*, a poetry collection immersed in the letters of Georgia O'Keeffe, is a great model for this exercise.) ■

Epistolary Works Recommended for Further Study

Barrett, Andrea. "Theories of Rain." In *Servants of the Map: Stories*, 99-120. New York: W.W. Norton & Company, 2003.

Munro, Alice. "Carried Away." In *Selected Stories*, 523-63. New York: Vintage, 1997.

Murakami, Haruki. "The Kangaroo Communique." *Zyzzyva*. Translated by J. Philip Gabriel. 8 April 2011. zyzzyva.org/2011/04/08/the-kangaroo-communique.

Robinson, Marilynne. *Gilead*. New York: Farrar, Straus & Giroux, 2004.

Schumacher, Julie. *Dear Committee Members*. New York: Doubleday, 2014.

Smith, Lee. *Fair and Tender Ladies*. New York: Putnam, 1988.

HOPE IS A THING
BEFORE FEATHERS

A wren hops twig to twig
to twig
in the long winter

hedge, a pulse inside
a maze of scratches.

Scant leaves catch rain
that starts to fall in thicker
slants of silver as

dusk
absorbs the wren.

In April she was inside an egg.
The rain was just noise
and her throat a pipe dream.

LAURA LONG

DAMSON

Consider the soft indigo body
the wax bloom
wrapped around amber

a drupe—
tender flesh, clingstone.

a tear, a bite, a rush of indelible sweet-tart
this is how sunrise fills your mouth,
the morning a reverence
of tongue and swallow.

EILEEN ELIZABETH

BOOK REVIEWS

Fenton Johnson. *At the Center of All Beauty: Solitude and the Creative Life.* New York, N.Y.: W.W. Norton & Co., 2020. 238 pages. Hardcover. $26.95.

Reviewed by Jayne Moore Waldrop

Fenton Johnson's new book *At the Center of All Beauty: Solitude and the Creative Life* launched a day before the World Health Organization declared a global pandemic due to the novel coronavirus disease outbreak. Life changed quickly. The subsequent shut down altered our busy lives and routines in ways we've never experienced before. Schools, restaurants, bars, bookstores, libraries, sporting events, malls, and other hubs of human activity closed. We learned to social distance as the primary way to stay healthy, stop the spread of the virus, and flatten the curve. We tried  to adjust to a world suddenly in a much tighter orbit with more time alone than we normally choose.

Undoubtedly the circumstances were not ideal for a book launch, but for readers the confluence was fortuitous—the release of a beautifully written guide to solitude just as we were told to stay home. Reading *At the Center of All Beauty* during the pandemic provided unanticipated comfort. Johnson portrays the solitary life as a chosen path, "not as tragedy or bad luck or loneliness." He uses the word solitary, adopting the term favored by the Trappist monk and mystic Thomas Merton because it is free of gender, sex, or negative connotations. Descriptors such as spinster, bachelor, single and loner come with baggage, where "[s]olitude and silence are positive gestures."

With impeccably researched details, Johnson analyzes the lives and work habits of well-known solitaries and how their creative work required discipline, stillness, and separation from conventional societal expectations. Separate chapters study Henry David Thoreau, Emily Dickinson, Walt Whitman, Paul Cezanne, Zora Neale Hurston, Eudora Welty, Rabindranath Tagore, Nina Simone and other kindred souls in their preference toward solitude and its fundamental role in their artistic genius. In stunningly beautiful prose that shifts between narrative nonfiction and memoir, Johnson takes the reader on a journey that spans centuries, continents, artistic genres, and spiritual practices, while weaving in his own story deeply rooted in Kentucky.

Johnson grew up on land near the Abbey of Our Lady of Gethesemani, a Trappist monastery set among the knobby hills near Bardstown. His Roman Catholic family with nine children had close friendships and working relationships with several of the monks, including Merton. Despite coming from a large family, from an early age Johnson spent "a great deal of time in the company of solitaries," from monks with their vowed solitude to his parents' personal variations on the theme. Johnson's parents carved out solitude within their traditional marriage. His mother spent hours alone in her greenhouse nurturing orchids and cacti. His father loved woodworking and built a simple cabin of reclaimed timber—his HERMITage— in the forest on a nearby Corps of Engineers lake.

Throughout the book there's a close connection between solitude, spirituality, creativity, and the natural world, but there's no exclusive path toward becoming a solitary.

> *Like getting married or professing a vocation to religion, living alone results from complicated, interlocking factors and decisions, made or avoided. Some of us were born to be solitaries—some were from birth 'not the marrying kind,' as my grandmother so presciently said of me....Many of us have arrived at our solitude as a result of circumstance— as who does not arrive at any place in life as a result of circumstance? Some gave our hearts away, to find that once given away they were not so easily recovered.*

Johnson notes that we live in an era with growing numbers of solitaries. Some choose solitude for spiritual, creative, and intentionally contemplative reasons. Others grew up regarding solitude as a homeland, as outliers and outsiders, due to race, sexuality, or class. Some are shy, widowed, or divorced. As societal expectations of conventional marriage or other coupling are abandoned, there's greater freedom to make the choice to live alone.

> *We are in the midst of a demographic revolution whose long-term implications may be as significant as the twentieth century's mass migration from the countryside to the city. I speak of the astonishing numbers of people worldwide who are choosing to live alone or who deliberately carve out periods of solitude from otherwise conventionally coupled lives. The evidence is accumulating that when people, especially women, are presented with the opportunity and the means to live alone, many will sacrifice to seize it.*

Johnson views the phenomenon not as a sign of a crumbling society but as "the potential for more diverse and loving relationships to one another and to our planet." Another modern trend—the barrage of background noise in our lives like Twitter, Facebook, texting, and other nonstop media—drowns out the true issues of our time, from environmental devastation to the growing gap between rich and poor.

As with Johnson's previous works, especially his memoir *Geography of the Heart*, this book takes the reader on a journey away from fear to a broader understanding of the human condition. *At the Center of All Beauty* becomes a guidebook on how to live alone, even how to die alone. Both are powerful lessons, particularly during a viral pandemic that altered our daily routines and changed our circumstances. Those who naturally tend toward being solitaries will find generous fellowship in Johnson's descriptions. Others may find new ways to see and perhaps embrace these unexpected paths toward solitude.

Jojo Moyes. *The Giver of Stars* New York, N.Y.: Pamela Dorman Books, 2019. 400 pages. Hardcover. $28.00.

Kim Michele Richardson. *The Book Woman of Troublesome Creek.* Naperville, Ill.: Sourcebooks 2019. 320 pages. Hardcover. $25.99.

Reviewed by Donna M. Crow

The Pack Horse Library Project was a Works Progress Administration program that paid (mostly) women with no other means of support $28.00 per month to deliver books to remote areas in the Appalachian Mountains between 1935 and 1943. Riding horseback (or mule) these women delivered more than books. They brought hope, human contact, education, and mental escape. Buried in history, relatively little has been written about them. In 2017 *Smithsonian Magazine* highlighted the horse-riding librarians as the Depression Era's first mobile library. In 2018, NPR's *Morning Edition* produced an episode entitled "The Pack Horse Librarians of Eastern Kentucky." And in 2019, two new Kentucky-based novels were published: *The Book Woman of Troublesome Creek* by Kim Michele Richardson, released in May; and *The Giver of Stars* by Jojo Moyes, published in October. Finally, the literary world seems to be catching up.

Richardson's *The Book Woman of Troublesome Creek* is told first-person through the eyes and voice of nineteen-year-old Cussy Mary Carter. Nicknamed "Bluet" for her cerulean skin, she is one of the rare "blue people of Kentucky" carrying a genetic trait for methemoglobinemia. Townsfolk, even Cussy's fellow librarians, see her as the "other", sanctioning a thread of racism that drives the storyline. Pushed deep into the mountains to avoid prejudice, Cussy uses isolation to learn self-sufficiency. Her vernacular is thick and betrays her intelligence, allowing her cleverness to be overlooked in favor of condescension and judgment.

Cussy's burdens are loaded from the beginning, with a concerned father whose misaligned attitudes on gender force her into an arranged marriage to an insensitive opportunist many years her senior. She is used, traumatized, and impregnated by her husband and then accosted by his cousin, a self-proclaimed preacher, who justifies his own evil behavior via the misguided religious notion that her skin color makes her a sinner. Cussy's inner spark and desire for independence, her care and attention to her patrons on the library route, the unlikely friendships she forges, keep us rooting for her as she drudges forward and overcomes obstacles.

Written in close third-person, Moyes's *The Giver of Stars* weaves in a braided narrative the voices of several women who become a team of librarians, relying on one another for support. Two main characters, Margery and Alice, an unlikely pair, drive the plot as they forge a bond against all odds. Margery is a self-made hardscrabble native whose deceased father was a bootlegger and outlaw  which is enough to brand her a scorned woman. With that distinction, she seems freer than most to do what she likes, albeit discreetly. Alice, a demure English woman, is new to America, having married the son of a rich coal baron. Her expectations of luxury and freedom are dashed after he moves her to a small rural community near the mines where she finds just as many, if not more, limitations. Through the individual and collective relationships of the team of librarians, readers experience a force of woman power and the truth that it really does take a village.

Unfortunately, once Moyes's novel was set to be released, rumors began to flow that portions of her story may have been "borrowed" from Richardson's work. This suspicion, reported by *Buzzfeed*, was alleged by an advanced reader/blogger who'd previewed Moyes's book in April, then alerted Richardson—before either book was released. Richardson, a talented but lesser-known author, was understandably alarmed when *Variety* announced the bestselling British author's *The Giver of Stars* had already been optioned by Universal Studios.

According to *Buzzfeed*, Richardson claimed plot points of *The Giver of Stars* were "alarmingly similar" to those in *Book Woman*, which were fictitious and original to Richardson's imagination, not founded in her extensive research. I believe her plot points were original. But it's not a far stretch of any woman's imagination to envision some of the hardships and obstacles an Appalachian woman in the 1930s would encounter on backwoods mountain trails. There are too many women with similar real-life stories to believe one imagination won't resemble another.

Both books are easy reads with memorable characters; however, neither book is remarkable for its unusual plot points. The underlying themes are similar in that both books address misogyny, racism, poverty, the breaking of old customs, and the empowerment of women against all odds. Stories as old as the hills, though each author brought to the page unique characters to tell their own.

I haven't met Kim Michele Richardson yet, but I met Jojo Moyes when she came to Kentucky to research *The Giver of Stars*. Perhaps it was a CNN documentary on Beattyville, Kentucky that inspired her to act on her impulse to visit Kentucky firsthand. She interviewed locals, listened to dialect, heard stories, and found the voices and relationships of her "library women." She rode horseback through Cumberland Mountain trails to get an inkling of the terrain her literary army faced. She visited Louisville's Free Public Library, one of the first libraries in the nation to be fully operated by African Americans, where she found one of her characters, Sophia.

Not unlike the novel's author, the transplant character Alice falls in love with Kentucky and its people, and it is her English voice that lends credence to the authenticity of an Appalachian story written by someone from afar. Through her eyes we see ourselves as others see us, and through the voices of the women she loves, we hear our own. By her capable hand and particular care and respect, Moyes has earned her place among writers of the region. The biggest flaw of the novel is Moyes's casual use of geographical locations and rural road names. Her multitudes of far-reaching followers won't likely have noticed, but for me, it was jarring to see characters traveling routes in a span of time that would not have been possible, or to read that the Ohio River had flooded an eastern Kentucky coal mine.

As for Richardson's *The Book Woman of Troublesome Creek*, I appreciated the attention to geographical details, as well as the savviness of her mountain characters regardless of dialect. This is an authentic narrative for Appalachian people and Richardson, a Kentucky native, gets this part right. However, the sophistication of Cussy's literary knowledge, given she is supposed to be self-educated with no formal instruction, feels stilted at times, as if we can hear the author coming through. Regardless, Richardson lends an authentic voice with attention to detail in a colorful story that illuminates well-researched historical facts.

Perhaps the bright spot stemming from the controversy over these two novels is that the readership of both books will increase out of curiosity. Both books are entertaining and educational, and both are worth reading.

Keith Maillard. *Fatherless: A Memoir*. Morgantown, W.Va.: West Virginia University Press, 2019. 240 pages. Softcover. $23.99.

Reviewed by Katie Mitchell

Keith Maillard's memoir *Fatherless* explores the void left when a father is absent and the insatiable curiosity that grows as his son searches for answers. What begins in his Vancouver kitchen with a simple phone call from a stranger to explain that his estranged father has died becomes a meandering journey to discern precisely who this man was and why he was so reluctant to call Maillard his son.

The result is a book that is sometimes heartbreaking, often lighthearted, and always honest. An experienced novelist, Maillard manages to examine the roughest edges of his family history with harsh truth without begging for the reader's sympathy. What emerges is a portrait of a man who may not have fulfilled all of his son's needs but who was a vibrant presence in the lives of many others nonetheless. Maillard pieces together the fragments of a father who holds the key to his own history but stands as a complete stranger. He handles this complexity with a narrative voice that is many things at once—curious and angry, reluctant and voracious, soft and brutal. As the pages progress, an experience that begins with bitterness eases to a more tender portrait of a man who lived his life with full and round possibilities and, like the rest of us, didn't always make perfect choices.

While the memoir begins in Vancouver, it winds itself through decades of history and miles of territory to land in

Maillard's native West Virginia. The distance between regions and cultures mirrors the distance between the writer and his father. He reconstructs not only the history of a person but also the history of a region and a time that is long gone. What results is a study of working life in the early twentieth century and the people who stem from it. Sketching the lines of his father's character, Maillard fills in the colorful pieces as they are revealed to him in interviews and letters. He searches for answers with a sharp tenacity and interviews his father's old friends, former students, coworkers, fellow Masons, ex-wives, and anyone else who can help him better understand where he comes from.

A musician and a tap dancer with a distinct youthful bravado, his father becomes a character the reader approaches with fascination and frustration. The central tension in the book stems from the ways Maillard finds mirrors of his own experiences in his father's life despite his resistance to these similarities. They are both artists, one a writer and one a musician. They both had periods of feeling lost and untethered. And eventually, they both settled into solid lives as their fragmented pieces came together.

The story can be heartbreaking at times, but Maillard keeps his distance, even calling his father *Gene* as he writes, always holding him at arm's length. Readers who crave a memoir with more heart will sometimes become frustrated with his journalistic approach to reconstructing his father's character. Between the lines of this distance, we feel the sting of his unanswered questions. He does not idealize Gene, but instead he leads us to see him as a man made of flaws resulting both from his own making and from the time and region that built him. Maillard's prose refuses to shy away from the truth of his discoveries, but never once does he paint this portrait with oversentimentality. The journalistic style becomes less apparent as the pages progress, and we see a rejected son reckon with the rejection of a father who didn't measure up to expectations. What is unsaid often speaks louder than what is directly stated in this memoir, and Maillard does not blur the edges with description and softness.

In the end, we are left with an honest record of a forsaken son coming to terms with his troubling father's actions, the void those actions left behind, and the echo still ringing loudly for Maillard himself. Those of us who have lost people we love without receiving all of the answers to our burning questions will find a mirror in Keith Maillard's words, and others of us will see ourselves in the telling of this tale as we all eventually cross that threshold between perceiving parents as infallible creatures and seeing them for what they really are—real people with flaws and lives that began long before we ever existed. Maillard tells us, "Trying to read my father into my life, I'd been forced to read the absence of something rather than the presence of something. I tried to read the blackness of the shadow—to read what wasn't there—because nothing was there." *The blackness of the shadow* and the richness of what Maillard constructs from that darkness are what readers will remember most after they turn the last page of this memoir that reveals how even a distant son can give voice to the fullness of his father. ■

WHAT I COULDN'T GIVE HER

Two large peach cans beneath a one-inch-thick board
fronting the cabinet doors, the kitchen sinks above,
a platform that supports me so my elbows clear
the sink's top edge. Through the bedroom door behind me,
mother in bed with the flu or a migraine, wavers in and out of sleep.
I ply the water, more bubbles for dishes and play,
until she calls out my first and second names.
I couldn't see my toes then. I couldn't see above the sink.
I couldn't see the mimosa tree that mother hadn't planted yet,
beyond the window, it's sweet pink. I couldn't see
the long barn on the hill we would build about ten years later
with our own cut lumber. I couldn't move without teetering off
the peach cans. I was sure I was the orphan brought in
to do the work no one else will do—this scene repeated
so often while mother's pregnant with her fourth,
the only one she wouldn't be able to breast feed
of the six of us. I would give her my two peach cans
but then I couldn't reach the dishes
and what would mother do then.

MELVA SUE PRIDDY

THE KITCHEN, EMPTY

All hands at work in the fields, our house cool, maple-shaded,
I stopped for a glass of cold water, or maybe it was supper chores,
when I heard their peeps, like tin bells, jangling between my small steps.
Behind the table, the cabinet, the folded towels: the garden box.
The pink hairless thimbles, hunger nested in shredded paper,
seed's warmth. I knew what they'd say. I closed the box,
tucked it under my arm, took father's boot in my hand.
What I want you to know is, I had to. That the screen door clapped
as I walked to the burning bin. That I did not look again.

MELVA SUE PRIDDY

CONTRIBUTORS

Jason B. Crawford is a Black, bi-poly-queer writer born in Washington, D.C. and raised in Lansing, Michigan. In addition to being published in online literary magazines, such as *Wellington Street Review, Barren Magazine, The Amistad,* and *Kissing Dynamite,* he is also the Editor in Charge for *The Knight's Library Magazine.* His chapbook collection *Summertime Fine* was a Short List selection for Nightingale & Gale.

Donna M. Crow, a resident of Estill County, Kentucky is the third generation to live on her family farm. She writes fiction, creative nonfiction, and poetry. Her work has appeared previously in *Appalachian Review, Still: The Journal, Now and Then, The Minnetonka Review, The Louisville Review, Blue Lyra Review,* and other publications. She received her MFA in Creative Nonfiction from Spalding University.

Benjamin Cutler was raised on a riverbank. His poetry has been nominated for the Pushcart Prize, Best of the Net, and has appeared in *Cold Mountain Review, Pembroke Magazine, The Shore, The Carolina Quarterly,* and *The Lascaux Review,* among many other publications. Cutler is also a father of four and a high school English and creative writing teacher in the mountains of western North Carolina. His debut book of poetry, *The Geese Who Might be Gods,* is available now.

Kathleen Driskell is Chair and Professor of Creative Writing at the Spalding University School of Creative and Professional Writing and is the author of four books of poetry. Her collection of poems *Next Door to the Dead* is the 2018 winner of the Judy Gaines Young Book Award. Her poems have been published in many national journals including *Shenandoah, the Southern Review,* and *The Louisville Review.* She currently serves as chair of the board of the Association of Writers and Writing Programs.

Eileen Elizabeth is a queer Appalachian essayist and poet. As the cofounder of *Boshemia Magazine,* she directs a UK/US print magazine and digital platform focused on amplifying the voices of LGBTQ+ and nonbinary folks. She is currently an MFA candidate in Nonfiction at the University of California, Riverside.

Ansel Elkins is the author of *Blue Yodel*, winner of the 2014 Yale Series of Younger Poets Prize. Her poems have appeared in *The American Scholar, The Believer, Oxford American, Parnassus, Virginia Quarterly Review*, and elsewhere. She has received fellowships from the National Endowment for the Arts, the North Carolina Arts Council, the American Antiquarian Society, and Bread Loaf Writers' Conference, as well as a "Discovery"/*Boston Review* Prize. She is currently Visiting Assistant Professor in Creative Writing at Berea College.

Amanda Greene grew up in Atlanta and then traveled west to attend Art Center College of Design in Pasadena. Greene's work has been published in *The New York Times, The Oxford American, Garden & Gun Magazine, Aint – Bad Magazine*, and featured on *The Bitter Southerner, The New York Times* LENS blog and *Looking at Appalachia*, and has been exhibited at The Museum of Contemporary Art of Georgia, Hathaway Contemporary Gallery, The Swan Coach House Gallery and Slow Exposures.

Angela Jackson-Brown is an award-winning writer, poet and playwright who teaches Creative Writing and English at Ball State University in Muncie, Indiana. She is the author of *Drinking From a Bitter Cup, House Repairs*, and the soon to be released novel *When Stars Rain Down*. For more information, visit her website at www. angelajacksonbrown.com.

Sheila R. Lamb received her MFA from Queens University of Charlotte. Her writing has appeared in *The Anthology of Applalachian Writers, Rappahannock Review, Monkeybicycle*, and elsewhere. She lives, teaches, and writes in the mountains of Virginia.

Laura Long is the coeditor of the anthology *Eyes Glowing at the Edge of the Woods: Fiction and Poetry from West Virginia* (West Virginia University Press, 2017) and the author of two poetry collections, *The Eye of Caroline Herschel: A Life in Poems* and *Imagine a Door*, and a novel, *Out of Peel Tree*. Her writing appears in *Shenandoah*,

Southern Review, and other magazines. She teaches at the University of Lynchburg in Virginia.

John Q. Mars is a Black and Queer writer, with four poems in Indolent Books's online feature, *What Rough Beast.* He is twenty-one and was born and raised in Winchester, Virginia. Mars is now an undergraduate student at New York University, living in Brooklyn. He is majoring in Linguistics and studies poetry and foreign languages.

Katie Mitchell is an English teacher and a North Georgia native. A 2019 participant in the Appalachian Writers' Workshop, she is currently at work on her memoir, *The Shape We Leave Behind,* and represented by Folio Literary Management. She lives with her two children in Cumming, Georgia.

Melva Sue Priddy's poetry places a reader in rural Kentucky from 1950s to the present. A life informed by land and family, the slow coming to terms with the physical and emotional work of that life mingle with the healing power and experiences of earth and nature. Priddy's work may be found in *The Louisville Review, Poet Lore, Still: The Journal,* and other publications. She lives near Lexington, Kentucky.

Mark Powell is the author of six novels, most recently *Firebird.* He has received fellowships from the National Endowment for the Arts and the Bread Loaf and Sewanee Writers' Conferences, and in 2014 was a Fulbright Fellow to Slovakia. In 2009, he received the Chaffin Award for contributions to Appalachian literature. He holds degrees from Yale Divinity School, the University of South Carolina, and The Citadel. He lives in the mountains of North Carolina, where he teaches at Appalachian State University.

Emry Trantham is an English teacher in Western North Carolina, where she is raising three daughters and writing poems. Her poetry has been published or is forthcoming in *Tar River Poetry, The Adirondack Review, Noble Gas Qtrly, Cider Press Review,* and other publications. She is also a 2019 Gilbert-Chappell Emerging Poet.

Jessie van Eerden is the author of three novels, *Glorybound, My Radio Radio,* and *Call It Horses,* winner of the 2019 Dzanc Books

Prize for Fiction (forthcoming in March 2021). She is also the author of the portrait essay collection *The Long Weeping*. Her work has appeared in *Best American Spiritual Writing, Oxford American, Image, New England Review*, and other magazines and anthologies. She has been awarded the Gulf Coast Prize in Nonfiction, the Milton Fellowship, and a Mid Atlantic Arts Foundation Fellowship. van Eerden holds an MFA in nonfiction from the University of Iowa and teaches creative writing at Hollins University.

Jayne Moore Waldrop is the author of *Retracing My Steps*, which was a finalist in the 2018 New Women's Voices Chapbook Contest (Finishing Line Press 2019). Her work has appeared in *Appalachian Review, Still: The Journal, New Limestone Review, Minerva Rising, Deep South Magazine, Anthology of Appalachian Writers*, and other journals. She lives in Lexington, Kentucky.